Advance Praise for *Fearless Teaching*

"Each story compelled me, challenged me, or just plain stopped me cold in my tracks."
—Clint Davis, Head of School,
Discovery Preparatory School

"Insightful, light-handed, and immediately appealing to any thinking person. It runs out to play in the woods beyond the backyard, but it always comes home."
—Doug Katz, Author, founder of JamArtz Studio

"Stuart Grauer is rapidly becoming one of America's most important and popular educational story-tellers. With Fearless Teaching, Grauer makes an invaluable contribution to the urgent conversation that we all must have if we are to successfully change the direction and substance of formal education. In Grauer's hands the 'story telling' directs us to crucial and well researched truths about education."
—Joe Brooks, Executive Director,
Community Works Institute (CWI)

"It is a deeply rich book filled with stories of hope, compassion, and curiosity . . . *Fearless Teaching* is a way of life—a challenge to us all to stay open, to play, to explore, to stay curious, to be happy and most importantly, to love."
—Michelle Rose Gilman, Founder,
Fusion Academy and Learning Centers

"Recommended for parents, teachers, school principals, and children. Want to change your paradigm? Go on . . ."
—Sugata Mitra, Professor of Educational
Technology, Newcastle University, UK

"*Fearless Teaching* is a unique, consuming, and transformative mediation on a pedagogy of listening that will reinvigorate our shared commitment. Trust Stuart Grauer."

—Chris Thinnes, independent school leader,
Fellow of the Martin Institute for Teaching Excellence.

"Each story is a gem unto itself—conveyed with humor, compassion, and deep reflection on the deeper meaning of 'education' in today's world. The global perspectives provide richly detailed points of comparison and contrast to American education ideologies. The Socratic framework models best practices for teaching and learning, and sustains ongoing inquiry long after finishing reading."

—Anita Charles, Ph.D.,
Professor of Education, Bates College

Praise for *Real Teachers*

"The point of Stuart Grauer's book is to remind us that Great Teaching, singular, rare, unusual, is something that should be sought after and found. Thank you. It's wonderful, timely, accessible, clear as a bell."

—Richard Dreyfuss, Actor, Oxford scholar,
founder of The Dreyfuss Initiative

"I will always love it."

—Deborah Meier, NYU Senior Scholar,
MacArthur Fellowship Award

"Must reading for all educators, regardless of their educational philosophy."

— Chris Mercogliano, Author,
In Defense of Childhood and *Teaching the Restless*

Fearless Teaching

Fearless Teaching

Collected Stories

Stuart Grauer

Stuart Grauer is the founder of The Grauer School and The Small Schools Coalition. He has taught all grades, elementary school through graduate and his awards include the Fulbright and the University of San Diego Career Achievement. Grauer's work has been covered by Discovery Channel and *The New York Times*. His previous book, *Real Teachers: True Stories of Renegade Educators* (2013), brings "joy, courage and imagination to the dialog on education."

Alternative Education Resource Organization
417 Roslyn Road
Roslyn Heights, NY 11577

Cover: Black Dog Designs
Layout: Isaac Graves

All photos courtesy of the author. Cover photo courtesy of Steve McCurry, one of the most iconic voices in contemporary photography for more than thirty years.

A portion of author proceeds for this edition of *Fearless Teaching* will be used in support of refugee and community education, including ImagineAsia.

The Gaokao Cowboy is a revision of an original article written for *Independent School* magazine, Summer 2015, Volume 74 Number 4.

Printed in the United States of America.

Library of Congress Control Number: 2015945205
ISBN: 978-0986016004

To the staff and faculty members of The Grauer School, for their generosity and purity of intention, and for their trust that our connection is more valuable than the best work of any of us.

"Want to change your paradigm? Go on . . ."

—Sugata Mitra

Contents

xvii   Introduction: An Open Field of Questions

1   Prologue: The Socratic Oath

*****

5   In Praise of Hooky

9   What the Revolution Looked Like

14   Kindness

19   An Alpine Idyll

25   Begin and Begin Again

41   Tikkun Olam (Healing a Fearful World)

52   The Triumph of the Revolution

61   Five Karibuni Stories (School Hopping in Tanzania)

65   Extinction

69   A School Where the Old Village Acacia Tree Once Was

79   Blessing the Goat

87   How Do You Educate a Warrior? (Emboreet)

97   Unschooling

109   A Gateway

115   Samaya (Teacher and the Parent)

123   Navajo School (How Miracles Happen)

131   Still We Can Wander

135   Pete Seeger: A Real Teacher

143   The Wounded Ones (A Winter Night With No Lights)

149   Zenbells (The Art of Paying Attention)

155   The Gaokao Cowboy

165   Too Nice a Day to Stay Inside

171   Tree Stumps

181   What Do We Care About?

185   Boulder

191   Han (Happiness as a Measurable Educational Outcome)

199   Education in the *Real World*

203   What the Revolution Looks Like

209   Find Your People

219   The Manhasset Indians (Lacrosse and the Real History of Comprehensive Schools in America)

229   Bigness (We've Got to Fight, Boys)

237   The Black Horse of Tahiti

243   Indians of Six Nations

247   The Moon in a Jar

253   A Refugee

*****

259   Afterword: About These Stories/*An Origin Tale*

265   Bibliography

271   Follow-Up Questions for Socratic Seminars and Groups

279   Acknowledgements

Do not depend on the hope of results . . . you may have to face the fact that your work will apparently be worthless and even achieve no result at all, if not perhaps results opposite to what you expect. As you get used to this idea, you start more and more to concentrate not on the results, but on the value, the rightness, the truth of the work itself . . . you gradually struggle less and less for an idea and more and more for specific people . . . In the end, it is the reality of personal relationship that saves everything.

—Thomas Merton

One of the President's new schools. Outside Arusha, Californian and Tanzanian students form a circle for song and dance.

"Stories can serve as powerful organizing tools for neural network integration. A story that is well told, containing conflicts and resolutions and thoughts flavored with emotions, will shape brains and connect people."

—Louis Cozolino

Introduction
An Open Field of Questions

Can we restore story to a world obsessed with data?

A few years ago, while this book was still just a few sketches, I met a teacher from Surry, England, who described our field's basic conflict this way:

> Teachers start feeling like their own stories don't matter and that their primary role is in reacting or responding to the inspectors' standards. But when people are given a little time and space to do something creative on their own, you can't believe how excited and productive they become.

Tom's story captures a conflict that can play out in contradictory ways. Like so many of our students, many teachers feel marginalized or trapped, like an underclass, and they either resign or remain passive. Other teachers feel a calling, more than ever, to give generously if not unsparingly, as this field often demands—to find freedom for the expression of human spirit. This conflict is universal inasmuch as it transcends boundaries of all kinds, be they political, social or economic. Rich school or poor school, in any hemisphere you'll find stories where people live and teach in this bind, or somehow beyond it. But you don't need to travel the hemispheres, because you can read and ponder these Socratic Stories. As these conflicts find either resolution or dissolution in the following pages, meaning and purpose unique to every reader will emerge. Each *Socratic Story* in this collection resolves in paradoxes or questions that you, its reader, face alone. They may leave you a bit off-balance. Nevertheless, I think you will find a few of them that are good companions for you.

David Brooks wrote, "Once people start speaking to each other and telling stories to each other, they generate alternate worlds. A story isn't an argument or a collection of data. It contains multiple meanings that can be discussed, questioned and reinterpreted." In our data-obsessed field of education, telling us more of the same and confirming more of the obvious, a good story allows us to see the world through clear lenses, and to ask bigger, more humble, and more open questions.

As teachers, generation after generation, we see our findings cycle and recycle. In the current generation, we hear we need brain researchers to study the cortexes of baboons only to tell us that good teachers create the conditions for learning and don't stress their students out. In matters of the human heart and mind, though the answers may shift, the questions endure. Questions are our common ground.

These *Socratic Stories* are intended to challenge our deepest assumptions about what we do as educators (and students and parents) every day as we face the largest questions our field has to offer. Is the role of the teacher to civilize and dominate our students or to enlighten and empower them? *Is our teaching an act of liberation or control?*

Read the stories in any order you like. *Fearless Teaching* pulls from experiences from my own childhood and extensive public and independent school experiences, then moves out into the world further than I imagined I would, in an effort to listen better, and in this way to discover always more essential questions to ask. Years of searching for answers yielded bigger questions, and here are the biggest ones I could find:

- What if we evaluate our students and our schools by measuring happiness? Or kindness?
- Are we willing to risk our jobs in the pursuit of real and deepening connection with our students?
- Can open-heartedness prevail over the exhaustion and self-interest we often find around us?
- *How do we manage to stay in this work?*

The study of these questions keeps taking me back to a single question and many of the stories in this volume may lead you to it as well. It's a simple question, Socratic, hence, inviting your answers:

- *What greater expression of human freedom could there possibly be than teaching?*

Panamanian girl in Bocas del Toro paddles to school one morning.

Prologue
The Socratic Oath

What if teachers had their own Hippocratic Oath?

Friday morning. Bocos Del Toro, Panama. Neil set out from the dock at Bahia Honda in a panga half-filled with grinning, coffee, indigenous kids.

They headed out to a distant point where the surf breaks across a long, clean punta. Neil was a surfer of ability, taking off in critical spots, and moving up and down the face of the wave with precision while generating impossible acceleration. As such, he knew this point like few others.

All the way along, the shorelines were covered in impenetrably thick, green mangroves. Steering closer to shore, they eventually began to notice occasional dark spaces amidst the wiry and gnarled banks and, closer still, they appeared as tiny, green, creek mouths; as slight inlets big enough for a few dugout canoes. And closer still, a few little ones running and chasing one another and grinning with delight as they flipped off the end of a dock. The Ngöbe kids of the Bahia Honda on the northeastern corner of Panama were waiting for a ride to school.

Behind the mangroves protecting the shore, with machetes, the Ngöbe had hacked thatched-roof, stilt houses, and extended family clearings of usually less than one hectare into the bush. Surrounding each clearing was wild and twisting, tropical overgrowth reaching to a high canopy and the best way you could describe this is with a word that some surely think is outmoded: jungle. Comical sounds floated out at various times of the day and it was hard to tell the forest canopy sounds of the monkeys from the birds or cicadas. Everything, including eight-foot leaves and nearly microscopic bugs thrived in this wild. Savage rains. Some strawberry poison dart frogs crawled around the base of a ficus tree, while a three-toed sloth hung from its top branch. Cocoa and cinnamon grew wild. In the Bahia Honda even the little ones began learning the skills of hand fishing. At five-years-old they learned kayaking, at seven, machetes.

At the next stop, Neil learned that the older, elementary school-aged children were not coming that day. Their two teachers were to be attending a government meeting . . . No matter, it would have been a rough ride for many in the rain, especially for those who paddled their dugouts to school.

He and his students arrived at school with a few preschoolers and, in the corner gathering area, a group of mostly female, pre-med students from Yale and Stonybrook, was convened. They were getting instructions for vaccinating the locals and dispensing vitamins and medication to ward off parasites. Seeing opportunity, a couple of them wandered into the schoolroom to show the little ones some medical tools. The rain was clattering down so hard on the metal roof that it was hard to hear anything else. Even so, the kids were captivated. A visitor watched from the teacher's desk and tried to take notes but termites were excavating the wood all over the writing surface and leaving piles of sawdust.

One co-ed pre-med student had a song about washing hands and everyone sang along. The ancient physicians' Hippocratic Oath was playing out before their eyes, and all these students, from preschool to pre-med, were filled with purity of intention: "First, do no harm," the oath implores.

What if not just physicians, but global aid teachers, inner city teachers, and every teacher on Earth could understand this oath? This would be the Socratic Oath: **"First listen. Observe. Prevent no learning."** Curiosity about our students will always provide greater wisdom than we can ever bring in. This philosophy restores our profession to its noble roots, and distinguishes the **teacher** from the **trainer**. As Socrates and every great teacher since has implicitly understood: teaching is the study of the student. This is where we must always start.

Behind the mangroves, the elders don't think much about the alphabet. They can only stand by in faith as their indigenous languages give way to Spanish, and even English as a third language. Worldwide, most of our students, and their parents, have little or no control over the education that is delivered to them. Down in Bahia Honda, Neil wanted to do what he could to connect this community, so that they in turn could teach themselves. But, in schools, not just primitive ones, including those across our own country, we have imported a lot of damage to our students by not listening to the communities that support them. What would our teaching in Panama bring to this ancient culture? Do they have some intimation of how unimaginably vulnerable they are now that the teachers are here?

Students follow Navajo guide in Canyon de Chelly,
New Mexico—the walls are textbooks.

"Freedom is the oxygen of the soul."

—Moshe Dayan

In Praise of Hooky

How can we teach freedom within the confines of the school and classroom? Is freedom ours to teach?

As a kid, I learned about playing hooky from the television characters "The Little Rascals," also referred to as "Spanky and Our Gang." For the gang, playing hooky meant skipping school and, typically, going fishing instead. In a memorable episode of the show, a truant officer, really a slapstick buffoon, busies himself by chasing one or another hooky-playing little rascal but never catching any of them. But then, none of those rascals ever caught a fish either. By the time I was seven, I was schooled by that gang. So when my mother walked my brother and I to the bus stop for our first, dreaded day of summer school, no sooner had she disappeared then we beat it on down to the woods behind our house, wandering all day long and, with perfect timing, reappearing near the bus drop-off at the end of the "school day."

The good-naturedness of these seditious memories, their freedom of spirit, provided me with formative impressions of schooling that influenced my childhood approach to education and persist in my nature to this day. Thus, my daughter Audrey and I played hooky once per year when she was in her earlier years. Not fishing. But Disneyland.

The routine continued for over a decade. We'd rise before dawn, drive to Anaheim and be the first in line. We'd burst through the gates at opening time, practically running down Snow White as she stood there greeting all who entered, running unbridled and irreverently past "Great Moments with Mr. Lincoln," and on to Adventureland. We'd run, never walk, from ride to ride. This was freedom, pure.

Once when a parade crossed our path on the way to Pirates of the Caribbean, we dared to join the troupe as though we were legitimate Disney characters, marching out in front, and just for that moment, we presided over a world of colors and motion, feelings and free thought and then, grinning and pumped, dashed out of the parade to land in the Pirates line. We paid mercilessly though when Audrey, only six, was terrified of the scalawags and sword-wielding, one-eyed captains. No matter. We escaped the ride, ran all the way to "It's a Small World," and were healed in a world of giant, plastic flowers and auto-animated dolls singing and frolicking in the spirit of international unity.

Year after year this was our one-day respite from educational incarceration, our anecdote to sitting disease, our liberation from the rows and columns we refused to let define us. We were connoisseurs of un-schooling! Never mind that I was a school official and supposed role model, I tried mightily to corrupt my daughter of the notion that schooling was not an act of free will. To hell with conventional wisdom about formal education; at least once per year we knew a world of playfulness with no experts, paragraphs with no topic sentences, and games with no officials. One in which we discovered our own patterns. Then back to school the next day with gleams in our eyes.

Now, many years later, I still wonder how, as teachers, we might find ways to add just a few such open spaces—little, renegade pockets of freedom—right in our own classrooms.

Kids not quite in dress code, Nanjing #1 School, China.

"If you want your children to be intelligent, read them fairy tales. If you want them to be more intelligent, read them more fairy tales."

—Albert Einstein

What the Revolution Looked Like

As teachers, do we sometimes become so preoccupied with our own agendas that we forget to ask our students for theirs? Are we so driven to deliver the requirements that we honestly feel we have no time to listen?

A good many people Tony Stone graduated Syracuse University with went into teaching. The career path came with a military deferment, meaning you got to stay out of Vietnam. He didn't really need the deferment though since he drew a high number, 257, in the draft lottery that took place in his sophomore year. Whew! The teaching market Tony was destined to enter though was glutted already because a lot of his fellow graduates drew less lucky draft numbers. For them, teaching was a more sensible path to avoiding Vietnam than was defecting to Canada or acting insane. And so because of this glut, it took him such a long time to get a job that he just about left the profession.

Tony's first big public high school teaching position felt like a miracle and maybe he should have lost it. He came close. At the end of the first year there, his principal called him in and said he would have to petition to stay because his students had not distinguished themselves on the New York State Regents examinations in the area of social studies. Additionally, he pointed out, the district was anticipating layoffs and Tony was ripe to be picked. If that had happened in today's educational environment with pressure on teachers to march through a controlled curriculum and produce predictable test scores, odds are Tony would not have even been allowed to petition. That would have been that.

But Tony, there in the principal's office, wisps of his long-curly hair left over from college running out over his collar, received all this news eagerly.

The petition to keep his job focused primarily on the various special programs he was always developing. This focus most likely saved his job. For instance, one time he created a program called "World Week," where each day a featured event addressed a global concern such as hunger or population. To this end, he contacted the office of the local U.S. congressman and asked if he would speak about nuclear power generation. "Nuclear waste lasts 10,000 years," he explained. Were we going to put it on the moon?

A couple of days later, he got them on the line again. They said the congressman would love to come out, but he did not care to talk about nukes. He wanted to talk about another issue of the day, the tragedy of the Vietnamese boat people. Nam was over, Saigon had fallen, and the social and political structures over there were a wreck. Vietnamese people were doing anything to get out of the country, even if it meant being packed like sardines into unsafe boats and shoving off for America. Ultimately, a quarter of a million boat people died at sea.

Tony thought, yes boat people was an important humanitarian issue. But his heart was set on the nation's energy future more. The Shoreham-Wading River Nuclear Power plant located right on the Long Island Sound was near his school and in the late stages of completion. Community opposition to the plant had passed the 50% mark. (Ultimately, that six billion dollar plant would never operate a single day.) So he pressed for the congressman to discuss nukes. The congressman, Tom Downey, who was himself only 26 years old, surely thought Tony was merely politically driven. This was not the case at all. Tony was nowhere near being that politically sophisticated. But the nukes seemed like something in his own backyard and the people protesting them seemed like him, like maybe friends.

Back in the faculty room, some of the teachers in the social studies department snickered openly at Tony's idealistic, un-gradable visions and the off-the-clock time it took to implement them. They'd come through an epic, 40-day strike just the year before. They still maintained an invisible picket line and he was crossing it. In the end, the congressman's office and Tony struck a compromise. He agreed to come out and speak about nukes so long as he could cover boat people as well.

A congressman was coming! The principal and assistant principals pow-wowed, quickly arranged for a whole school assembly, and alerted the press that something significant was going on at school. They were covering two big global issues: energy use and refugees. The union leaders pow-wowed as well, but for different reasons, and Tony would wind up walking around for some weeks with that vulnerable sense you get when people are whispering about you. "Watch your back," the elder guidance counselor told him, kindly.

The big day came. There was Congressman Tom Downey, young and handsome and filled with esteem, greeted by the school administrators. Tony shook his hand and took his place in the large auditorium with his class. The congressman spoke for a while, covering all the ground as agreed and, at the end, asked for questions from the 500 assembled students.

No one seemed to know what to ask. Why had everyone presumed that kids cared about the issues that burned deeply for so many, issues that suddenly seemed to be of concern for only an older generation? The Beatles had already broken up. These students were a new generation, one with an undiscovered voice. People were turning their heads from side to side looking for someone to speak up. To Tony's left sat a slouching kid with long, tousled hair from Tony's western civ class, Gregory, and just the week before he'd blown the clutch in Tony's old Skylark. So he owed Tony one. Tony gave Gregory a stern nod. Gregory raised his hand to his shoulder, then up ear-high, and the congressman nodded to him for the last question before returning to classes: "So, like, are they gonna' legalize pot?"

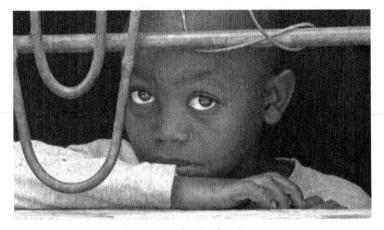

Tanzania boy on site of a school under construction.

"Be kind, for everyone you meet is fighting a harder battle."
—Plato

Kindness

Hundreds of research studies document how nearly half of all teens feel hopeless, depressed, or alone at some point during the school year. Are teachers, parents and policy makers responsible for this? What aspects of school and classroom organization cause isolation and cliques?

Years later, hardly any of us would even remember the British kid who came to our school and then was gone. The memories are fragments. His baggy clothes and his strange, worn leather briefcase. His unusual complexion. Nobody'd ever met a British kid before and no one thought to even talk to him. There he was, leaning back against a wall, alone, chin down, eyes narrowed.

From those junior high years, and even through high school, there are few things I came to really regret. Surely not the fight with Billy Green behind the bus stop as everyone watched on. Not that D in typing—that would become a good story at the reunion. And surely not getting sent to the principal's office for wearing blue jeans. Few of the kids would ever regret those extra laps coach made us run after gossiping in PE class, and I know for sure that none of us will ever regret going surfing instead of going to class some afternoons in senior year.

But seeing this boy every day and never saying a word to him, turning away, huddling together with my little pack, and even taking comfort in this huddling in full view of that British kid alone at the bus stop that day . . . seeing him trying to blend in to the brick wall, then getting on the bus last . . . Probably told his family at dinner time, "Yes, mum, 'course I have friends."

And then one day he was gone. That's what I regret.

A guide moves students through the Boundary Waters, Canada-Minnesota.

"I stand before you as one who offers a small message of hope . . . there are always people who dare to seek on the margin of society . . . and prefer a kind of free-floating existence under a state of risk."

—Thomas Merton

An Alpine Idyll

Beyond our lesson plan, without the curriculum and the room, are we still teachers? Does all our training leave us with something essential that defines us as "teacher?" Is there a place for wisdom in school, or for elders?

Once, six of my students and I traveled with a group from Bern, Switzerland down to an alpine village. We bunked in a massenlager and from there we would set out early the next morning on a trek. We woke up pre-dawn, along with a few members of the Bern section Swiss Alpine Club, and then roused the students. Hardly speaking a word, we moved quietly to the trailhead, stuck our sealskins onto the bases of our skis, and began our ascent. At that time of year you could see well enough a good 30 minutes before sunrise, and not long after we could see shadows beginning to turn into dull, bluey colors. We wound our way up the trail as the trees thinned out.

The first destination was to be our guide's house, high up on the Bunderspitz. This was the easy leg of the journey; not too steep or complex. Soon after dawn, we reached the mountain guide's farm chalet perched on the high mountain pasture. He was a fit, thin, older-age farmer with whispy white hair, translucent-whitish and leathery skin, and sparse facial hair that looked like it had been cut with a knife and no mirror. We all bellied up to his long, wooden table for muesli. He had only two spoons so the eight of us passed them around. Afterwards, we gathered our gear for the rest of the trip.

Setting out again, our guide, the old man we had only just met, led us up higher, making our way towards a small pass. Moving through in a line, we entered a cirque, which looked something like a crater, and began crossing through it. We passed little brooks and grey rock formations, but it was mostly flat until we reached the other side. In front of us rose a formidable set of crags, which were the highest peaks on this mountain called Engslingenalp. It was late winter and we had expected to be comfortably warm, especially after having hiked a while when our bodies would have heated up from the trekking. But that wasn't the case. Cool, crisp snow swirled around so we kept our jackets fully zipped and some of us even strapped on goggles as we plodded behind our guide picking his way up switchbacks, around rocky outcroppings, and across small chutes and snowfields towards the summit.

I was young in those days, and my mind jumped about, leaving my body to plod along impatiently and uneasily. Starting on that very first morning, I began realizing this from an unlikely source, the old man. Though he looked too frail to me to be doing this ascent at all, it turned out he could hike the whole day, patient and peaceful, while

I, supposedly young and strong, dragged behind while wrestling with my own mind and muscles. He had a sense of humor about most things and kept a gleam in his eyes as each knee pressed forward with the opposite side ski pole in a slow, eternal glide.

At last we arrived at the summit. We clicked out of our skis and took our treats from the backpacks. A wedge of cheese, block of chocolate, water. I tried to swap English for Swiss-German swear words with the old man tit for tat, just for a challenge. But I didn't stand a chance. Swiss German is a very old language.

Someone had brought a bottle of wine for the occasion of this summiting party so we celebrated for a short while as it got overcast with mists moving in right before our eyes; a sure signal it was time to leave. We peeled the sealskins off our skis and locked in the heels of the bindings.

The first section the old man chose to lead us down was not the usual roundabout way we had taken on the way up, but rather a steep, small cliff. Why had he chosen such an expeditious path? I no longer remember the guide's name, but I will never forget the madly intense yet calm, knowing smile in his eyes as the weather continued to change.

Now we could see only a few feet ahead. One after another, each of us jumped down this chute until the group reformed and was ready to start the glide down in unison. Descending from climbs like this is the most beautiful experience in God's creation if the snow is good. There's a sense of floating in snow, the shushing sound, the rhythmic breathing, the slow motion bouncing and springing down the mountain face and across the snowfields. It feels like freedom. We all lived for that, but now the snow was swirling much more and the fog was dense. So increasingly we tightened our formation, each of us trailing a long red string behind us. This was well before the days of reliable avalanche beacons. We were on our own.

We made a little progress, yet were still towards the top of the peak, far above the floor of the cirque, and the snow was swirling madly now. My eyes were deceived by the illusion caused by gusting winds and I remember thinking, "The snow is falling up rather than down." We could see almost nothing and lined up together much more tightly. It was intensely obvious to me that without the old guide we would be completely stranded. But he lived in this area, farmed in this area so I felt comforted some as we followed half-blindly.

Descending, making small tight turns to control the downhill speed and keep the formation, we alternately stemmed and picked our way further. When it's wild like that, snow being swept in all directions, it's hard enough even to balance or orient your body. You press on though. The question of whether you are getting out of the situation or further into it lingers, and you never really know where the end will be. It is a good time to have a teacher you trust, even one who says almost nothing.

Then the steepness leveled off and we began working our way across the flatter area. The guide methodically picked his way across the cirque and, somehow, through a pass, and down to the lower face of the mountain until, at last, we arrived in the tiny Swiss hamlet for coffee, raclette, eggs, and bread with thick pats of butter.

In our school, almost always whenever we go traveling, we use local guides. Local wisdom is a form of knowing that cannot be centralized or standardized, cannot easily be written down and is often unknown until it is needed.

Today, in education, a set of big government and corporate teachings are prevailing. Who knows the place for local or elder wisdom? If there were a local expert in our community, their knowledge would likely be considered as marginal in most of the schools, amidst the swirling storm of national and international "standards." Any student with enough intuition to find a unique path would likely try administrators' patience.

And yet I have no doubt that students suffer daily in the world's classrooms for lack of what those intuitions have to teach us all, and the lack of old men and women. The idea that a teacher is a guide with some special knowing, something akin to wisdom, is viewed as arcane and too unreliable to allow in the classrooms of America. And we will never keep up. Instead, we stay in this storm, and the idea that there is even a way out seems like a dream. We are expected to make our students be in a safe place where all knowledge is known, and to pretend that this is the path to all places worthwhile. A wise guide might feel terribly lost in a world like that.

*Author by statue of Confucius in front of
historical Chinese high school testing site.*

"The time will come
when, with elation
you will greet yourself arriving
at your own door, in your own mirror
and each will smile at the other's welcome,

and say, sit here. Eat.
You will love again the stranger who was your self.
Give wine. Give bread. Give back your heart
to itself, to the stranger who has loved you ..."
—Derek Walcott

Begin and Begin Again

How real are the lines on your resume? How much of ourselves dare we reveal to our students? What does it mean to be a teacher?

However pragmatic and explainable they may appear, many of our life stories may be traced back to mythical or epigenetic origins, like Homeric or even primal tales of long ago. The ancient tales are woven into every field of endeavor. If only we can access them. Here is the true story of what happens when two teachers on wildly different journeys eventually meet. Each one speaks in his own, unique voice, faithfully recorded herein:

The First Teacher

My path to teaching was straightforward. As a small child, I was mild mannered and compliant, liked by teachers. I minored in education in college, and went on to receive teacher certification and a master's degree in education. From there it would be a steady advance. I taught at a New York City prep school, specializing in art history and world history, then moved to the suburbs and was tenured at a large, comprehensive public school.

Next, pursuing a global perspective, I taught at an international school, eventually apprenticing myself to the headmaster as an administrative trainee. At age 29, I was put in charge of another international school, the youngest principal in the European Council of International Schools. Again parlaying my experience, I selected the University of San Diego (USD) School of Educational Leadership and spent five years earning a doctorate, my third degree. While there I conducted market research on the potential for an independent school. As a next step, I began teaching at graduate schools of education and then, networking with education professors, founded an independent school start-up based on the principle, "learn by discovery." I employed the best principles from academia and the California State Curriculum Frameworks and, before long, we received our accreditation. The school grew every year for a quarter century and evolved into a permanent campus of stature, yielding me honors, awards and worldwide friendships, including the University of San Diego's alumni career achievement award.

Ultimately I taught for over 30 years in schools large and small while also consulting and serving as an accreditor for schools all over the world. These building blocks reveal a logical series of achievements, plotted out assiduously. But the global perspective and "learn by discovery" themes permeated every phase of school and career development.

Taking stock, I presented my resume to the school board: 30 years of persistent commitment to the education field, primarily working with adolescents and a school that had grown every year. I had fared well. A sabbatical was granted. In preparing, I transferred many of my duties and responsibilities to other offices, passed along hundreds of file folders, and at last turned the key in for my office door, untethered and with no intention of returning predictably to a teacher's desk the next week for the first time in three decades. With automobile mapping programs logged in and calendar marked off, I packed up a van, and headed south for 19 solid hours. Deep in the desert, at last, I would meet the person who would transform my life.

The Second Teacher

As a small child I was visited by a long series of night terrors, and it took me 50 years to see how this made a teacher out of me. The subject of the terrors was this: I was inside a shadowy cave, which encased and entrapped me and yet, paradoxically, was infinite. This is, of course, impossible, but paradox lives well in dreams. Over a period of a couple years, I awoke repeatedly to this same terror screaming and flushed, sometimes in a bathtub, as my parents attempted to bring me to consciousness, and eventually I began learning something only dreams can teach us: the contents of my own subliminal thoughts. These terrible dreams figure significantly in my memories of being a child and of, later, exploring the human netherworld that became my subconscious mind.

My path to teaching was nonlinear, appearing differently from every angle. I drifted through school fairly unconsciously, preferring to be outdoors. In college, I did not plan on going into teaching and have no recollection whatsoever of what caused me to sign up for a course in education or to eventually minor in the subject. I did not distinguish myself in those courses, though I did receive an A in my final one as a result of an offer the anti-Vietnam War professor made: if you showed up for the final you aced it.

During college I also signed on to the audio-visual department and they randomly pegged me to show the weekly slides to art history classes.

My first "permanent" full time job was in a fine, upper East Side Manhattan Prep School. My resume made no mention of my prior jobs fishing for lobster many miles off of George's Bank in the North Atlantic, or pumping gas or flipping burgers. When I arrived in New York City, I discovered that, although I had studied little in college, I could accurately name and describe most of the contents of the Metropolitan Museum of Art. I roamed those halls in wonder, astonished at my own recall of years of art history slide shows I had never thought much about. With this curriculum vitae, I was assigned the job of teaching art history.

A few weeks before concluding my second year in this school for the privileged, I literally shipped out to pursue a dream, sailing the great Atlantic on a topsail schooner. Fired from my teaching job upon my return, I quit the profession to become a writer. "I can teach a thousand people that way," I told my father.

Before long, however, a public school offered me a job, part-time. I had forgotten I had even applied there. (Simultaneously, I received an attractive offer to be an international appliance salesperson, though my mother lost the phone number of the person who called.) And so I became a teacher again.

I moved out near the school and soon found myself walking into a neighborhood bar. After winning a few rounds of pool, which irritated a small motorcycle gang, several thick and leathered bikers jumped me and pounded me into the floor. The next day I again wandered into the bar and asked for a job. I told others this job was to supplement my income, but I knew it was really my way of walking into fear. "Still not mellow?" my childhood friend Peter said to me, and even I wondered if I'd ever grow up. (I wouldn't.)

It did not take long for me to feel boxed in at my new school. There were testing requirements, union reps, entrenched unwritten rules, and a preoccupation with the pension plan. Public regulations prevented me from taking my students anywhere, but I brought fascinating people into the class almost weekly—chefs, NGO reps, politicians and artists. Anyone to help merge the classroom with what seemed real.

My daily commute to the school was on long flat plains, and I developed a habit of imagining the clouds as Alps. As if I were escaping my childhood nightmare, I envisioned skiing high and free and my imagination and life vision became entwined. My life path was guided by instinct and, at best, intuition and never a plan, which would have been too committal. Late one afternoon I wandered into the Jaunting Car Pub and at the urging of Beth the bartender, put down a ten for the Superbowl pool. I won. The next I day purchased a plane ticket to Switzerland, where I met the headmaster of the International School of Bern. We corresponded for four years until I received the following telegram, the only telegram I have ever received: "Dear S-, We have a sudden and unexpected opening to teach at the International School of Bern ..." I was gone.

My first season in Bern, I developed what I called "the off-piste ski group," the goal of which was to take students skiing freely out of bounds, on unmarked Alpine mountainsides.

There in Europe, being a teacher seemed to have an older, broader meaning, and I came into contact with other educators who, to my fascination, had actually started their own schools. That one could do this had never crossed my mind, but it tapped into something inside of me. For reasons I could not at the time explain, almost instantly, starting a school became my dream, like a pulse that beat inside of me.

Visiting family in San Diego one summer, I woke up one morning and, with no plan or intention, drove to The University of San Diego. There I met the advisor who tapped into something older in me, as though he were a part of my lineage. Dr. Joseph Rost was to become a part of the ground upon which I would build a school. "I might start a school," I told him. I made no applications elsewhere, and knew little of the philosophy, reputation, or potential outcomes of this program. I completed the requisite paperwork and testing and was admitted. Hence, I would leave Europe.

I arrived in California without a penny in my pocket. On my very day of arrival back to America, I started in the doctoral program. I had swapped the alpine dreamscape for the unfathomable lure of the Pacific Ocean.

When people look at The Grauer School now, beautiful, pristine, and green, they often assume it arose from a place of privilege. Nothing could be more wrong. I spent many years teaching in the public schools. Upon graduation from my doctoral program, I had no plans, no business experience, and still no money. And yet I sensed that this lack of everything was my greatest asset. Call it openness. I had been working at an independent school where the grandfather of a student said to me, "There is a 'for rent' sign outside the Rincon Plaza that I pass by every day. Why don't you stop in there and see if you can rent your own classroom space?"

So I did. Unable to pay rent, I got the landlord to lend me the space until I had some students. To this day I find that, all over the world, people open doors for me and the only code for entry is, "I am a teacher."

I also stopped throwing out the incessant junk mail I was getting offering me credit cards, and replied to them until I had seven. I was rich. I took my cards down to Target to purchase school supplies, filling up two shopping baskets, which I took back to the storefront, and began outfitting my two-room school.

Taking a break from assembling cheap furniture, I sat out in front of my new school on the curbstone, well before I had even a single student, and felt a stirring that I could never have predicted. There, alone, I felt less lost than I had in all of my "real" school experiences. I had purchased an American flag on an impulse and, suddenly, was overwhelmed by the largest picture I could think of: In America, one could freely start a school.

Heart pulsing, I hung the flag on to the front of the building, then went inside and booted up my computer. A blank screen appeared, and that was the canvas on which the school would take shape. My computer was a first generation Mac and one of the standard font sets included graphical icons from which the only conceivable, useable one was the globe. So I set this globe image into the header. Imperceptibly, unthinkingly, I hit the return key and observed myself typing, underneath the globe, the phrase: "Learn by Discovery," as though it had been there all along.

I treasured those days of approaching work as a Tabula rasa, an open world to create, off-piste, but we were poor and I had to moonlight as a college professor. Some of our students were "privileged" and I was passionate about showing them corners of "the real world" that could awaken their compassion.

Our school sought accreditation and, before long, two very skeptical officials came by and sized the situation up. I soon received the following letter which, still today, framed, remains by my desk: "Dear ... We regret that we do not find your model of a school to be accreditable and we advise you against pursuing accreditation status." But we kept trying.

Twenty years went by and the school kept growing as we experienced every possible phase of organizational development, each one seeming logical only when it was over. And so it was that, after what felt like a lifetime, a bit exhausted, I presented my resume to the school board of trustees: 30 years of persistent commitment to the education field, primarily working with adolescents and a school that had grown every year. I had fared well, despite a few quiet pathologies picked up along the way: shingles, bradycardia, and a penchant for grasping the steering wheel too tightly with my right hand on long drives. I proposed a paid leave characterized by only hints of requirements or agendas beyond the pursuit of open space. A sabbatical was granted.

Before I knew it, I was turning the key to my office door for the last time for the next six months. I was a little lost and with utterly no intention or plan but open-mindedness. I set out, driving 19 hours south of the border, for a remote spot where I would spend 40 days and nights alone to surf and write and begin again.

I thought I would be alone. Then one day, I recalled my ancient terrors. "Have you ever felt in conflict with yourself?" ponders Jon Kabot-Zinn, and I knew I had been my whole life. At last, the first teacher described earlier, the teacher of record, came face to face with the second teacher, the shadow teacher, and I was no longer trapped alone in the box. Years of searching schools all over Asia, Africa, North American and South America and across the oceans and now I could see, as the prophet Ezekeil found in his journey and as the cliché now goes, that the journey is of course inside of us. "Wherever the spirit would go, they would go, and the wheels would rise along with them, because the spirit of the living creatures was in the wheels" (Ezekeil 1:20). The years of public achievement at last confronted years of conflict, drifting, avoidance, and failure. These two selves had threaded tightly together and now they were unraveling. The startling, unexpected allure of an American flag came to mind. At last unbound, I understood that it was never a teaching career I had been pursuing, it wasn't any career. It was freedom.

*****

"Eat," poet Derek Walcott encourages us. Once we invite the forces that guide us subconsciously to enter into the story of who we are, we have the opportunity for congruence. "You will love again the stranger who was your self."

Most of us are fearful to access the shadow self because it reveals our vulnerability, lack of control, and dependence. We replace curiosity with a set of presumptions. Our ego takes over. The word "should" creeps deeper into our daily vocabulary and our teaching. Over time, we ignore the subconscious scripts that dictate to us how we define our "selves" or our profession until they are buried. Who we are or could be is replaced by presumptions of who we should be. We don't want to give up our great resume, however artificial it seems. And then, like it or not, one day we become aware of how very scripted we are. We may or may not be looking for this. We may be driving, or reading, or walking—or teaching—and this realization comes upon us like a traveller. Perhaps we let him in.

The Teacher

> The second night there, far out in the desert, the farthest I'd ever been from another American, the electricty, hence the lights in the village, all went out. At nightfall, I walked out on the deck of my house and felt the soft air. With a new moon, there were no streets or lines or neighbors, only the village dogs to howl of the chaos and directionlessness. The night sky was so clear and sharp that the stars seemed like pinholes drilled through the ceiling of a Baja cave of unbounded proportion. There was absolute quiet with the sound of the ocean breathing just a few blocks down. A shooting star slipped beneath a constellation I could not name, so quickly I was not sure I'd really seen it. I realized with a smile now that I was holding my breath trying to capture what was not there and that there was nothing to capture, no shooting star or cave, no metaphor, and nothing there to separate us.

Congruence starts when we make intimate disclosures to ourselves: our fears and foibles. And then to others. We risk being known. We confront the rules of rank and status, willing to let them go. Through this vulnerability, the façade of independence collapses and the space for humility opens up. In this space, we better sense how infinitely bound we are to those around us. We can at last make peace with how interdependent we are, how reciprocal everything is. With others. With our own shadow selves.

We are sure of our calling once everything in the world relates to it. Then our boundaries become permeable and our curiosity about those around us becomes unhinged from our agendas and public image. Our vulnerability may expose our weaknesses, but it also awakens our hearts to face others in the most genuine way. The awakened teacher embraces the occasional chaos of not knowing where the lesson will end, feels unburdened by stodgy old authority systems and untethered by the geographical location of the school—but remains confident in the capacity and depth of students. From then on, our real school is anywhere new thought, creativity, responsiveness, and connection occurs among and between students and faculty.

We will always confront, even within our own selves, the resume builder, the compliance driver, and the distant, self-absorbed professional, along with the wild fallacy that our help is more valuable to others than it is to our own selves. We recognize these ego-people when we see them, of course, and can sense their conflict sometimes mildly in their hurriedness, other times overtly in their diagnostic approach to relationships with students and colleagues. Of course, they are us.

The disconnect comes early in life, when we join the educational competition that honors high scores above genuine relationships, creativity, and peace of mind. Schooling can sever our minds from our souls, and as teachers we can spend our entire careers trying to re-attach them. Once we meet ourselves, we rediscover trust in our intuitions, in our curiosity, and in our students. Coincidences, hunches and insights become a part of our daily lives as they were when we were small children, and so we invite them into our classrooms.

Eventually, we may open up the door to a set of presumptions that look pretty much the opposite of those with which we entered the profession; and we can discover a new definition of teaching: the study of the student. Acknowledging our dependence upon our students and fellow teachers reveals our deepening interest and curiosity about them. We shift our approach from didactic to Socratic.

Following our curiosity about how our students approach a topic or subject can become a fundamental and endless source of fascination, even though it sometimes does not pay off. This, in turn, opens the door to authentic and more intimate relationships where students can become more curious about their teacher. In this same way, we can discover new definitions for service: the study of those we serve. We can redefine school site leadership as the study of the leaders around us, our faculty, or our team.

Our greatest teachers do not criticize our ideas, however bizarre they are—they only ask to know more. Sufi teachers refer to this as "the wisdom of the idiots." Over time, if we are lucky, we may learn how little we know, and this is the essence of Socratic teaching. We stop disguising our vulnerability and weakness, we sense that our view of the world is oblique and naive, and so we pursue our teaching and service as a way to access our own larger awareness and connection. The great teachers, it seems, are those willing to take off their armor and drop the role-play, at least from time to time. This is the field where we at last meet our own selves in the most natural way in the world, so that we can meet our students.

Israeli and American kids exchange text messages at Hand in Hand dual language (Hebrew-Arabic) school in Jerusalem.

"I have no personal animosity toward you.
I have just one goal, to get the right answer.
So I'm going to try a different approach.
I'm sending you to the bottom of the sea."

— Murakami Haruki

Tikkun Olam
(Healing a Fearful World)

The great martyrs and leaders through history—Socrates, Confucius, Jesus, Siddhartha Gautama, Mohammed—were all called "teacher." Who is called a teacher today?

W**e were on a sort of peacemaking mission, visiting schools in the Holy Land. I was trying out my new Canon Eos Xsi with image stabilization that week, too. I was thinking the camera might help me approach things as a dispassionate observer, that is, if anyone could be dispassionate on that land.**

By way of background, my father married a *goy*. (*Goy* is Yiddish for gentile.) In kind, as if to get even with the indignant in-laws, my mother married a Jew. In the hallways and athletic fields throughout high school, my identification with one religion or another ranged from neglect to ambivalence, except at times when I heard Jews mocked or scorned—which they were regularly in the town of Manhasset, New York. Only then, I became a Jew. As a result, given my flawed ambivalence, a vague religious identity was assigned to me in high school like a cross to bear, and I was the brunt of various forms of anti-Semitism and prejudice, an experience no educated person should be without.

After college, I began tinkering with Buddhist thought, which is practically a branch of Judaism for Baby Boomers and Gen-X'ers anyway. I liked that it was not really a religion, at least in my thinking, and through the teachings of the Buddha I could focus on peacekeeping for my own mind. In sum, I was born treading on borderlines, and the pursuit of incongruity has been a lifelong friend of mine.

So when we arrived in Israel I could feel an old stirring in me.

We were supposed to meet first with one of the members from Combatants for Peace, an organization of former Israeli and Palestinian fighters who have been imprisoned. But we learned that our assigned combatant was stuck at a checkpoint east of Jerusalem. The Israelis had closed many of the thruways because of a visit by President George W. Bush, so now we had extra time at the Western Wall. The "Wailing Wall," made of large blocks of Jerusalem stone, has been a site for Jewish prayer for centuries and was a great starting point. I got a photograph of an Israeli soldier in his olive-colored drabs with a Galil semi-automatic assault rifle strapped to his back putting on a disposable, paper yarmulke as he approached the Wall to pray. Afterwards, escaping the riot of ironies that could only be Jerusalem, we headed to our accommodations on a kibbutz, set on rolling, pastoral fields, where we got to look out upon the ancient lands of milk and honey.

Bright and early the next morning, we headed over to

the Hand in Hand School in Jerusalem. Hand in Hand is a program for mixed ethnicities featuring dual language immersion. Classes are held in Hebrew half the day and Arabic the other half. Our students dove in and gave English lessons and made artworks with the little ones. In one photo I took, a blissfully grinning middle school boy is gripping a classmate in a headlock—a clinch we, as kids, used to call "the Egyptian"—while the teacher wrings her hands before the whiteboard. Then we learned that the president's wife, Laura Bush, would be at the school the next day for a visit and that everyone must learn a dance to perform for the First Lady. The school development officer and the Bush handlers who were running all over the school had decided on us learning a particular folk dance to celebrate the 60th-year anniversary of modern Israel. We sloppily learned the dance, then raced off to play some basketball together. Later, I got an iconic, millennial photo of the older students, ours and theirs, gathered around, staring into their cellphone screens and text messaging one another.

After lunch, we entered old, walled Jerusalem along the Avenue Dolorosa, walking on the same steps Jesus had carried his cross. A shopkeeper with deep black eyes tried to bait me: "Bush is here" ("Booshe is heere"). He smiled broadly, sweeping his long, thin fingers across nuts, rugs, ram horns and crowns made of thorns as though he were conferring some kind of enchantment upon them. We had to get out of there early though since the traffic was backing up because of Bush.

The next day the plan was to cross over to the West Bank, a.k.a. Palestine or the Palestinian territories; a.k.a.

"Occupied Territory;" a.k.a. "Disputed Territory." What to call this dusty stretch of Earth is a classic lesson in multiple perspectives for our students. We were visiting the Dar al Kalima School, in Bethlehem, a stone's throw from where it is believed Jesus was born.

Some of the Jewish people in our party chose not go, for safety reasons, but as it turned out faith didn't seem to matter since at the checkpoint no one asked us what our religion was. Still, the security is intense. I felt weirdly vulnerable at the border, and actually started pondering if maybe they could somehow see through me. Did they have intelligence reports? Did they know that I am half Jewish?

I photographed the jumble of fences, radio towers and spotlights at the checkpoint. Then I got a picture of a giant sign reading "Peace Be With You" before the landscape transitioned into shabbiness with rubble, dust, and older cars. About half of our students said they felt safe.

Coming from a place of American privilege, I had felt stirred and exposed like this just the year before, visiting the Lakota Indians. They had never wanted to be Americans and were committing suicide at record levels. Now again, crossing into the disputed ruins of my very own ancient traditions, I felt conflicted and compelled. Who would deny a homeland for Jewish people after the terrible war? But then, who would deny the Palestinian people on the other side? Which side was the oppressed? Am I oppressed or privileged, a Jew or an American? And what is this irrational feeling of identifying with the oppressed on either side?

Across the border, once in the school, the principal

greeted us near a wall of Palestinian students' artwork. It seemed so typical of kids' art until we looked closely. One drawing depicted a machine gun under a heart. Another was of tanks and bombs, all in primary colors. We were told that many of these students had scholarships because their fathers were dead.

Like at the Jewish school in Jerusalem the day before, these Arab students were commemorating, too. For them it was the day of Nakba, which means "catastrophe" in Arabic. Sixty years ago, they are taught, their sacred land was invaded. And just as the kids on the other side, the Palestinian children are happy to see us and don't appear to presume anything at all about us. Don't they know we are Americans? How could they appear so innocent and yet create such horrible drawings of bombs and broken hearts?

I got a photo of a Palestinian high school teen in blue jeans checking out my own daughter, who I think was too young for him. By now I was loving how the camera lens kept freezing wildly conflictual, Holy Land moments like this, turning them into balanced aesthetics.

In music class, a drum circle started up and some of us joined in. The first drumming is of an old Lebanese folk song, round and slow. We became absorbed by the mysterious, droning sound of long ago:

> The girl over a grinding stone
> Imagines the old days, so beautiful they were,
> Green fields like a lullaby,
> So romantic,

Memories of grandfather working the grinding
stone.
How beautiful the old days,
Walking around the road, singing. Old times.

I was mesmerized. Afterwards, the teacher wrote out the music for me and now, back home at holiday time, we can form this same drum circle and feel this same ancient stirring.

Now it was time to commemorate al-Nakba. We all ambled out back behind the school to a bluff above the parking lot. In the photo I took, we are marching, carrying kites with colorful plastic sails under little puffy cumulous clouds in a baby blue sky looking out over a craggy, dirt hillside.

We all started setting up our peace kites. Students were to inscribe their own peace messages and fly their kites high on this hill, which overlooks Jerusalem. The student I am paired with wrote, "No occupation," on his paper, rolled it up, and slipped it into the tail of a yellow and orange, plastic kite. "What is your peace wish?" I asked him, through the translator.

"An enemy is someone whose story you haven't heard," goes the old Jewish saying. Is this the story we all must hear?

Kites of all colors shifted above us as he thrust his kite and upward it went to join the others, tripping about at the mercy of the wind. Off to the side, the concrete back wall of the school was dented and pockmarked. Everything seemed dusty and worn.

We boarded the bus and headed home, soon reaching the checkpoint. Back in Jerusalem, Bush was addressing the Israeli Knesset that day about the 60-year anniversary, so it would take us two and a half hours to drive home instead of one. "We have been deeply moved by the celebrations of the past two days," the President was saying. A grim Israeli guard carrying an automatic weapon entered the bus, then mumbled something in Hebrew to our driver. Our students remained upright and perfect, with flat affect, like they look in those senseless teacher training videos they show in grad school about best student behavior.

The next day, we visited the Sufi Abdul Aziz Bukhari, Sheikh of Uzbekistan. The Sheik's family came to Jerusalem in 1616. For 20 years, this sheikh lived in Southern California running a Dunkin' Donuts shop not far from Disneyland, a candy-colored fairy-tale land with four quarters that suddenly suggest to me the Old City in Jerusalem, with its own worldly, storied four quarters. They called him "Fast Eddy." But eventually he returned to Jerusalem to take up his family's ancient Sufi prerogative.

The Sufi poet Rumi is said to have whirled and chanted:

> Beyond ideas of wrongdoing and rightdoing,
> there is a field. I'll meet you there.

In this spirit, the sheik's group, Jerusalem Peacemakers, surrounded the entire walled city and gave it a big hug. He was a child of the 60s and of ancient times at once. He was a beautiful man with moist eyes who spoke to our students about peace and gratitude. In my photo, there he stands garbed in an embroidered mantle and cap, up in his loft right in the middle of the old walled city, surrounded by relics from long ago. We are all children of Abraham, the sheikh said.

We looked out upon all four quarters of the ancient city like a dream, unified: Jerusalem, its quadrants portioned out like mystic lands that make it possible. Up there from the sheikh's loft, we were above the strife and bitter conflict, in our minds we could fill the Holy Land with mystery and treasure: California students and the Sheik of Uzbekistan, peacemaking together. I heard he passed away last year. Could there ever be another peacemaker sheik like this?

Before leaving Israel, we visited The Mount of Beatitudes. There we read the "Sermon on the Mount," overlooking the Sea of Galilee, right where it is believed Jesus gave his great sermon. "Blessed are the peacemakers, for they will be called children of God." Who can say they know God outside of their own heart but, up there, Jesus was probably the wisest rabbi I could imagine. When you translate the word rabbi from Hebrew, which is what Jesus' followers called him, it just means teacher. "Art thou a teacher of Israel, and understandest not these things?" he asked the other rabbis. Looking back on a photo taken that day, it seems overwhelming to imagine Socrates, Rumi, Gilgamesh, and Jesus all in a long line of people called simply *teacher*, our invisible companions up there on the Mount.

It felt good, just then, to be a teacher, but it also felt confusing. In the context of the Holy Land, I felt exposed and identity-less. Stuart Grauer—my first name a tribute to a Gaelic heritage. My last name a relic from the Austrian ghetto of my paternal grandparents. I can only imagine what it is like for today's American kids, my students, descended from two or three continents and diverse ethnicities, as they attempt to establish an identity.

Year after year, teachers bring their students to the Holy Land to help them see the common roots, the shared, ancient humanity, even if it is blatantly disconnected and mired in war. Perhaps our search for unity is going to be futile. Our students learned how Jerusalem, translation, "City of Peace," has been ravaged by thirty centuries of warfare and discord. No wonder Israeli and Palestinian 13-year olds are diametrically opposed on political issues. It was all I could do in Jerusalem not to be diametrically opposed to my own self.

For their part, Israeli and Palestinian textbook writers each depict the other side mainly as refugees and terrorists. Not too long ago, Georg Eckert Institute for International Schoolbook Research developed a textbook of recent Israeli and Palestinian history for use by schools on both sides. Identical events are described on facing pages from each of the two cultural/political perspectives. The textbook provides a wide-open space in the center for students to write their own impressions of the conflicting stories. According to a report in the October 13, 2012 issue of *The Economist*, no school on either side has ever adopted the book. Too bad. Isn't the whole point of peacemaking, the whole point of education, the whole point of this life, to find wide-open spaces like that?

On our last afternoon, we took the bus to get some

shawarma, and I wondered, are these students seeing anything close to what I am seeing? In the classroom, I could manipulate the situation, but in Israel there were signals coming and colliding from every direction. We were having process sessions with our students every night, but the history and present state of Israel was so indefinable, so complicated, I hardly knew how to conclude. What, after all, was the lesson I was teaching?

Maybe that was the message. Maybe the question was the only real teaching. As our physics teacher Morgan Brown is fond of saying, "The trouble is that our kids think uncertainty is a mistake." Except Morgan is only half right. It's not just our kids who are too uncomfortable with uncertainty. It's most of us.

In schools, we tell our students that answers are things you put into questions on exams, that science experiments have prescribed findings, and that lessons end with a bell. Meanwhile, the universe and our "real world" alike speak in paradox and open-ended questions. We peer into its walls like a prism, and in its many faces we experience growth, joy and suffering. The rides just keep on going, and when we get off of one, we're already on another. How can we reclaim open space in our classrooms?

The last photo I took was from surfing some small, choppy waves of Haifa. It's often said that surfers are something like a global tribe. We paddle into almost any break anywhere in the world as though it were evidence of a unified world. We surf for "Tikkun Olam"—for healing a fearful world.

All things are connected to water, or so the ancient Talmudic wisdom has it. So after a long, red-eye flight back we arrived in Southern California and, before even showering off the Haifa salt that had dried on my skin, I went straight into the waves of my home break, as a sort of symbolic thing—surfing on both sides. The waves were steep, pitchy and unpredictable that morning and the water was cold and biting, not at all like you think of California. Unfortunately, I lost hold of my surfboard and it was washed in to shore while I was held under the churning water like a rag doll. When this happens you cannot fight, the force of a wave is too great. You can only quiet your mind, even smile a little and just surrender to it until you begin to see light in one direction and at last you know which way is up. When I got to the surface, I was so jet-lagged and sick that another surfer had to help me in. I wanted badly to explain my story to him, explain that I was not an unworthy surfer, but I'm sure I will die before he ever knows it. He was from another tribe. Or, perhaps I had lost faith that we will ever be listened to, any of us, and I knew what I had to do as a teacher.

I racked up my board to go home. Just then, the whole idea that we can take forces of nature and control them and make them conform to our will seemed ridiculous. You have to heal yourself before you start healing the world.

Visiting Cuban classroom took six months of petitioning.

"A few years ago I spent a day with children of the sea Gypsies, the Bajau people who live off Sulawesi in stilt houses set far into the water. The children were swimmers and divers, boaters and paddlers, rinsed with seawater night and day until they seemed half-human, half-otter. I asked what their childhood was like. The answer was immediate: 'Children have a happy childhood because there is a lot of freedom.'"

—Jay Griffiths

The Triumph of the Revolution

Can we imagine students and teachers being free and untethered to digital technology? Is it worth imagining?

I was almost late getting to the vans as they loaded up to take our students and chaperones across the California border to Tijuana International on our first leg, bound for Havana. I had taken a right rather than a left, to swing by one of the three, jumbo, chain drug stores in my neighborhood so I could get some Alka Seltzer. I wanted to be ready for whatever food and water came my way. Trouble was, when I got to the jumbo chain drug store, even with the clerk's assistance, I could not find an ordinary box of Alka Seltzer. I could only find ten boxes, in a glaring assortment of colors. In Cuba, only cigarette boxes would have this kind of variety in the shops. There were new Alka Seltzer types to cover every crazy condition one could imagine and I grew muddled and irrational as I scoured the five rows of shelves. Where was the classic powder blue and white box?

Anyway, we managed to depart on time, soon crossing the border, then switching our smartphones to airplane mode. We would be almost unreachable for eight days. This was to be an historic trip, as not only was access to Cuba still very limited for U.S. citizens, but we had to go to extraordinary lengths to get to see their schools and participate in classes. Cuba was loosening up with Raul Castro as head of state, and they were starting to do a bit more for tourist dollars than they would have under the ideological, lock-down days of his brother Fidel.

The first night in Havana, we walked along a main boulevard named Las Ramblas. A student needed a drug store. We wondered, what if there were a single, huge billboard entering our own town saying: "To the revolution, always!" and a picture of either a rock star or God, since some blend of these is the only way we could describe the way Cubans talk and feel about Che Quevera?

We strolled by people, from toddlers to the aged, hanging out together, playing games. We walked past a gritty pool hall and the corner bar with three dollar mojitos. Soon we reached the farmacia, a white-lit shop with glass cases running fore and aft down both sides. Except most of the cases seemed oddly bare to us. There were two thin aisles in the whole place, and a soda cooler in the corner. There in the first case were some indigestion tablets, just one brand, in a simple and classic powder blue and white cardboard box.

After three nights in Old Havana, we were acclimating to a certain absence of... we weren't entirely sure of what. America? At our nightly journaling hour, our eleventh grader Claya observed, "I'm really enjoying getting to know everyone in our group. I like not having the cell phone with me. I'd be here texting and checking it every second." Ninth grader Cameron added with a hint of attitude, "Yea, I actually have to interact with everyone in the group and try to be friends."

Everyone was nodding. To us, Cuba was becoming one of the increasingly rare places where our United States "smart" phones were deaf and dumb. Cuban cell service carriers hadn't cooperated with AT&T or Sprint, or virtually any U.S. corporation since 1959. Strolling through Revolution Square and slouching in a lounge chair at the end of the long days, it was peaceful without the niggling feeling that there was something going on in that pushy, electronics netherworld that now resides permanently in some tiny corner of my brain. It felt like … freedom. "All of our input came directly from our own senses, and I think that's a fantastic way to experience a place," said our trip leader (and Spanish teacher) Mimi. Jonah, an eighth grader spreading out with classmates in the Park View Hotel lobby across from the old Presidential Palace, said the same thing, using other words: "I think I've learned three new card games."

In this non-commercial, non-connected, non-disruptive world we began reclaiming unplugged, uninterrupted time to check in not only with others in our group, but with ourselves. We wondered if our students understood the cause of this situation in Cuba: In 1959, western business and the whole of capitalist and corporate ownership was deposed on the island in what is known as the Cuban Revolution, but across Cuba is devoutly referred to as the "Triumph of the Revolution" (Triunfo de la Revolución). Fidel was already in prison and this whole revolution might have been avoided if Cuba's president at the time, Batista, had not been persuaded to let him out. And who did this persuading? It was Fidel's childhood teachers!

The students experienced all this triumph through the stark lack of consumer goods and merchandizing, a budding sense of what that felt like, and perhaps a deepened understanding of the '57 Chevy and its era, frozen in Cuban time. There was also live music at every single lunch and dinner: salsa/timba, tango, Afrobeat, cumbia, nuevo flamenco, Criolla and reggaton. Music playing, instead of streaming.

Hasta no necessito! "To not need," became our manifesto, shedding our consumer shackles. Students created and read rich journal entries of their observations and reflections, entries that may have been stifled within twenty words and engulfed by the abyss of Facebook back home. They wrote stories of entering the elementary school on the Plaza Viejo, of hearing the children in their red bandanas singing, "Fidel en la vanguardia de la juventud, Fidel multiplicado, Nuestro Partido Comunista!"

We think students are tethered to technology. But just what is it that technology tethers them to? The constancy of "interruptive technologies" can erode a child's independence, so the American child is under 24-hour surveillance. Nationwide, children grow up with the specter of mom and dad "looking in" all day. "I thought that tracking my daughter was just part of responsible parenting," one mom wrote to me. Now, far from home, in a communist country long known for the surveillance of its citizens, an unknown new land, we can imagine the sudden absence of electronic connectedness subjecting well-intentioned parents back home to a gamut of lucid and sometimes dark imaginings.

In our travels, we visited three schools. The Cuban kids struck us as focused, non-complex, intelligent, and sweet. We played baseball, the Cuban national game. We sang, drew, swam and connected easily, especially when compared to encounters we've had with kids from repressed, urban economies around the world. In some of those more "depressed" cultures, students seem more guarded and nervous in comparison to the Cuban kids we met.

One day we drove to a school on the outskirts of Havana and were introduced to Cuban kids in a biology class. They weren't all Cuban, though. Many were orphans from the former Soviet Union whose parents had died after the 1986 Chernoble disaster. They were Chernoble orphans.

The teacher, realizing a group of American students was a significant distraction, wisely cancelled the rest of the class and we all headed for the beach together. We arrived at a spectacular, secluded Caribbean spot. Fronted by white, silky sand and turquoise water, doubtless this would have been the snorkel beach of a Marriott or Hilton in most other countries, but here it was just an uncelebrated part of the school. A few students started meandering into the warm water. Then someone threw a ball in. Within a few minutes, most of the kids were lured in, forming a circle, moving the ball all around, splashing and smiling together. In education (and I guess in diplomacy), whenever and wherever a circle forms, and all eyes can meet, something good is happening. Then soccer lines were spontaneously drawn on the beach sand and more games sprung to life. It was good being out-of-range with kids, both Cuban and American, facing the millennial world, feeling free.

Abel was our Cuban tour guide. Every night after our touring, he and I ambled down the Agramonte, past the Granma Memorial, to Sloppy Joe's for mojitos, muddled the old way. They were cheap for me, but a mojito would have been two or three day's pay for him. There we sat in the newly restored luster of the very bar my own father frequented back in the glory days, and we talked about the old times and never the future. He strangely reminded me of my father. Some day the Americans will flood back in here with their Coke and Internet and who knows what will happen.

"This low-technology is having a liberating effect on the students. They seem inquisitive and open," I said to Abel.

He cited the great German pedagogue, Froebel, who invented the word *kindergarten*, and whose investigations showed how children learn more when they are adventuring, not tied down. "Play is the highest expression of human development in childhood, for it alone is the free expression of what is in a child's soul," he said. Singing, dancing, game playing and gardening were all part of Froebel's methodologies.

Upon returning, one of my colleagues, who sees things more politically than I do, asked me what it was like spending time with "people who lack individual sovereignty." I answered, "I don't know." The kids we met in Cuba were kids, straight up. Even small children can walk to school in the city without a cellphone as homing device and without leaving their parents in fear. And as Holocaust survivor and Grauer School emeritus faculty member Dr. Edith Eger has taught us well, it is astonishing how humans are able to create their own internal sovereignty to transcend tyranny and find freedom.

"Our senses were heightened down there," somebody said. How strange that these students had to come all the way down here, to a communist country, to get away from the constant surveillance of parents and schools in a wired nation. Could this be . . . the triumph of the revolution?

Welcome sign on traditional Maasai hut on the boma.

"A person often meets his destiny on the road he took to avoid it."
—Jean de la Fontaine

Five Karibuni Stories
(School Hopping in Tanzania)

What forms of teaching, schooling and culture are going extinct?

Introduction

The first President of Tanzania, Mwalimu Julius Nyerere was unique in eschewing titles like His Eminence or The Supreme One. He called himself "Mwalimu" or Teacher. Still today, "Mwalimu" (pronounced wolli-mu) is reserved for Nyerere as an honorific title. His successor, Jakaya Kikwete, was elected as President of Tanzania in 2005 and built 1500 secondary schools throughout the country, though he did not provide for the incidentals like books, paper and chalk, or teachers. What he did provide his people though was akin to space under the old, village acacia tree.

Who would want to give up the great sites and instead spend their days interacting in foreign classes with students in far-flung schools? This practice, which one might call *edu-tourism*, is sure to replace destination-oriented educational travel because students treasure nothing more than mixing it up with other kids. Whatever this practice lacks in grandeur or historical significance, it more than makes up for in the friendships, authentic interactions, and the rare insights it affords the educational traveller.

And so, in September of 2012, world religions teacher

Bill Harman and I travelled with eleven students, five chaperones, and two guides, school hopping in Tanzania. Shadowing Bill's posse was a Land Rover full of Maasai aides-de-camp, often wrapped in red checkered Shúkà robes, who worked hard at setting up tents and tending to the fires and goats, as they might be mortified to do back in the thorn tree rimmed bomas, homesteads where those jobs would have fallen to their wives. Back in the boma, work is mainly for women. But that's another story. Our guide, Killerai, said he'd rather push a Land Rover than make the trip in any other vehicle. And with that, we set off.

A young Maasai herder

Karibuni Stories
Extinction

It has long been believed by many that the purpose of the teacher is to pass along culture and tradition. What can we do if we see customs and traditions about to die in our own community?

After two days of travel and camping, we arrived at last in Moshi. Emmanuel, a physics teacher who lived in Weruweru which is outside of the town Moshi, was discussing what is important in a school, and he was using the exact word we had heard tribes use on two other continents: unity. "People only think to use the word 'Unity' when it has been at grave risk," I said.

At the time we were eating lunch with some teachers and students at the Weruweru Girls High School, in their compound not far from the foot of Mount Kilimanjaro. We had spent the morning embraced by the smiles, handholding, photographing and dancing of their students who had taken our students in as family and our teachers as world dignitaries.

Emmanuel smiled as his students dug in to their lunches. They were the most physical kids we had ever seen and seemed to live their lives holding hands. They could not get enough of holding our hands.

Weruweru has been designated as a UNESCO-affiliated school, as has our school, so we are sisters. Their students are selected by the federal government, and each family pays $50 for the 194-day boarding school year (15-20 more days than U.S. schools). That is the cost of a desk. Their average GPA is over 3.5 and their goal is the "A-level," the gold standard of the British examination system.

Emmanuel grew up in what he called the Barier tribe and spoke Barier at home. So did his wife. I asked, "Does your daughter speak Barier?" She was twenty and in college. He was proud she had gone to the University of Dar es Salaam, where the President of Tanazania went, and where he himself went.

"No," he said, "she cannot speak it."

"Why not?"

He explained she spoke Swahili. "It is the national language and she must know English in this world, too."

"How long has the Barier language been spoken in your tribe?"

"Maybe a thousand years."

"And it will be gone in a generation?"

Emmanuel shrugged. We dipped our fry bread and tried to finish up the beef and liver stew from the campus slaughterhouse in silence, the weight of the pending consequences of another language being lost too raw to talk about further. Not only would a language be lost, but history and song.

Soon it was time to leave Moshi and our students struggled as they released hands, hugged goodbye to their new friends, and loaded into the vehicles. We set out across town and looking through the van windows we saw people squatting in doorways, seemingly entranced, neither modern nor ancient, but somewhere in between western civilization and 70 million years of evolving life. The students grew quiet as they explored their own surprise and confusion that Wereweru students and teachers had created hope and even joy in this far away, seemingly third-world place. We had never had so many hugs. Why?

We woke up early the next morning in our forest camp to roosters sounding off combined with the melodies of Moslem prayer song as it floated through the community. We rose and tracked an eagle owl in the forest canopy before breakfast, and prepared for the day's trip. We would see seven schools that week and be met with karibuni in almost all.

Around the world, we continue to be amazed and enriched at the entrée, the grace even, afforded us for identifying ourselves as nothing more than "teachers". For all its wild variations, wherever we go, there is something unifying, something organic, about foregoing visits to national monuments and top tourists sites and, instead, just visiting local community schools and communing with the local students in them. Like the tribal languages and forest species, many small schools are disappearing. Go now.

Students in Emboreet treasure pencils and paper.

Karibuni Stories

A School Where the Old Village Acacia Tree Once Was

Will the teacher advance the goals of the state or is the place-based, local heritage equally worthy?

The Oraucha people are a traditionally nomadic, Maasai group of 150,000. Mostly herders, only a few of them have ever been in a school of any kind. We arrived in time to see all that changing.

Our Land Rover moves down a rutted dirt road, we pass two black-robed teens with painted faces, carrying spears, and exit the van to meet Alex Marti in his government-issue khakis. Alex, a powerful looking, soft-spoken man, was the Maasai tribal village leader in the Oraucha village of Olastiti, an outskirt of Arusha where urban life blends in with rural. Though villagers pay some taxes on goats, cows, and houses, the Oraucha Maasai get little in return for this. The government provides some courts and roads, but little more.

Olastiti was founded in the auspicious year of 1950, and it was named after the acacia tree that grew in the center of the village. "Was the school there?" we asked knowing that traditionally in African villages an acacia was the meeting place for school. Alex did not know. Besides, he was looking forward and thought it was time they built a school of bricks and mortar.

Like most acacia trees, traditional medicines are also largely gone from the cities of Tanzania. Maasai will travel all the way to downtown Arusha for pharmaceutical prescriptions to help with things like childbirth and malaria rather than drink tea blends of locally foraged herbs as they did for a thousand years. In addition, even though Tanzania has universal primary education, Olastiti kids have had to travel all the way to Arusha for secondary schooling. This is where Alex came in.

As in Detroit or Shanghai, Arusha students travel far to a mandatory, understaffed school, with few books. All over the world this challenge is similar. While the large, comprehensive school has become a place of hope for some, it has become incarceration for others. National day-long schooling, common among industrial nations, has obvious and profound historic merit.And yet, today it unquestionably disconnects children from local culture and its traditions. Day-long schooling diminishes the opportunity for children to play and explore, the most natural things in the world. In the comprehensive African school of today, instead of circles and clusters, we normally find rows. Instead of open spaces, there are calibrations of time. Instead of participating in a local village community and its language, students are often removed. Instead of learning from one another, children learn—and mentors teach—what is prescribed by the state. What will become of their precious, local languages and cultures?

For better or for worse, many of the Olastiti kids had

already stopped going to Arusha for school. According to Alex, they couldn't afford the bus fare. Stories circulated of how girls who could not afford the bus but wanted education were impregnated, exchanging relations with the bus driver for rides. (But then, we had heard the exact same story down in Arkansas, along the Mississippi, just a decade ago.) Other students tried hitchhiking every day, which was dangerous. Then, last year, Alex's dream of a secondary school right here in his village came true. Alex attracted a U.S. charity, "Achieve in Africa," to raise the building cost of $11,000, and the school was started. At first there were no chairs or desks, so the students sat on bricks, rocks and baskets.

*****

One morning, Alex walked us to the new school. Our group of eighteen California students and teachers moved through the village, down the goat trails with their five-year old herders, down the dusty streets of dirt and rock rubble; and past two thirteen-year old Maasai junior warriors carrying small wooden cattle-prods. Striking how their white face markings looked fluorescent in the sun. We continued past the orphanage, small farms and huts. Past a pool hall with a thatched roof. Donkeys. Tractors. We walked past harvested fields, and along the banana plantations. Bean, thorn, acacia and ficus trees line the fields. Chinese motorcycles were everywhere.

Is this a suburb? Even on the mud houses in this area, thatched roofs have been replaced with corrugated aluminum, so it must be. A hornbill flew overhead.

We walked about four kilometers, the same paths that students were now using every day to walk to school. We reached a ten-acre dirt and grass meadow ringed sparsely with thorn trees and a few cinderblock and brick homes, to arrive at the school on the far side.

Paulina Bagoye was the head of the Olasiti Secondary School, the first such school in the village. "Karibuni," she says, welcoming us all. She had a solemn, patient smile, close-cropped hair, and wore a simple red and grey swirled dashiki dress with matching sarong over her shoulder. She carried a flip-style cellphone in her hand. "Asante," we replied.

Her students lined up neatly before the school in their uniforms, facing us, and we scanned over them and out across the dry meadow where mothers and small children in colorful cloth drifted along the path carrying plastic buckets on their heads or backs. Young boys passed by herding cattle.

It was Saturday and some of the boys would not be herding goats or cattle that day. Some girls would not be fetching water that morning, either, because, even though it was not a regular school day, the Americans were coming. There were four classrooms for 211 students, providing class sizes typical for public schooling in Tanzania. Elementary classes can go as high as 100 students. They were expected to add more classrooms and there were plans for the school to double in size over the next year. There were four teachers provided through the Tanzanian government, each with a three-year college degree in teaching. They were among the less than one percent of students in Tanzania who go on to university

(Elimu Africa) compared to almost half of all U.S. youth and 67% of high school grads who go on to attend university.

No books or computers were in the classrooms. Students were becoming happier than they used to be though, explained Bagoye. She said the students were from 120 tribal families, of which 50 percent were Maasai.

As a gift, we had brought them white board markers, soccer balls, and Frisbees. What drove us to bring white board markers, I will never know. It was crazy. We should have brought them chalk. At any rate, most of what we brought them was for play. And what is more universal than play?

Somebody asked Bagoye about how she accommodates all the tribal cultures in school. She replied she saw no reason to teach culture or community values. Perhaps this is not what school is for since The National Ministry of Education provides the syllabus, and her goal is to deliver it. "Do the families teach local culture?" "What is the family role in education?" "Do you think the national educational program is a replacement for local and traditional cultures?" She had little to say about these questions, which remain and grow in their worldwide scope and periphery.

"We are happy," Bagoye reiterated. "We try to encourage our students to study hard." I recalled how, four years earlier while we were visiting schools in Botswana, the president expressed that the tribal people in the bush were a national disgrace, and should be eradicated. Tanzania's first president, Julius Nyerere, Mwalimu, role model for President Kikwete today, hoped to dissolve the differences between all of Tanzania's 131 tribes. Everyone would be more like one tribe he proposed. He called this "Unity." So it appeared that what I saw as colorful and irreplaceable tribal traditions were not valued. Bureaucracies prefer grey. Or perhaps I don't understand the whole concept of unity. Could "unity" really be any different than the march of virtually every human institution towards greater size, complexity, and demand on surrounding ecosystems? Does it really mean sameness or compliance? Or bigness?

Back home in the States, our federal government often engaged in programs similar to Tanzania's. Our program entailed the steady loss of local, place-based curricular decision-making in favor of mandatory, national uniformity. It took on names like Common Core State Standards Initiative or No Child Left Behind or even Advanced Placement. These were like gathering waves in a quarter-century old "accountability movement" in the U.S. Just like in Tanzania and many other countries, it had far more to do with filling projected job slots than advancing a rich culture or sense of community. Almost all the states had adopted these "standards." Texas and Alaska hadn't. They were still the wild west.

After some orientation we gathered all together in a large circle around the national flag for games of singing and dancing. No matter how lost or institutionalized we ever become with our students, being in a circle always seems restorative. Our students blended in, everyone holding hands and grinning. The flagpole was the new acacia tree—a central gathering place.

Next, as we had done in many cultures, the students

began kicking some soccer balls around. Once this happens, almost anywhere in the world, a circle begins to form and, from this, soon a game almost always evolves as people divide into teams and spectators. We had brought something new to them and, in a spin-off, we teased their curiosity with a Frisbee. Charlie, one of our ninth graders, tried to explain the point of the red plastic disc to our new friends, but after a few seconds of this the California kids just start tossing it around, demo-ing it. Everyone clustered, and the grinning locals began circling around and around in every direction looking for a pass, as we were all inventing a game. Amongst ourselves, we claimed to be the pioneers of a new sport in Tanzania. We were changing their culture! After a while, we had two games going on, soccer and ultimate Frisbee, each with its own spectators and cultural affectation.

On one side of the field, where a group of houses stood, small children had gathered fascinated by our skin, our Frisbee, and by the images we captured on the LCD panels on the backs of our cameras. Most of them did not appear afraid at all of their own camera images, as so many of their grandparents, the ones born around 1950 and earlier, would be. One, a little Moslem fellow, tiptoed up, peeked at the image, giggled, ran away, then tiptoed up to peek and run away again and again. I was surprised at the cultural diversity of these little ones. I think I was expecting an indigenous tribe here in the little village of Olastiti, at a time when many indigenous peoples were disappearing into a national or global blend. I am afraid that the Millennial world and its nationalized schooling systems are transforming cultures, and I feel a sense of loss.

Wood is giving way to plastic, color to dusty dun, circles to rows, space to time.

I thought about my own Austrian, Hungarian, English, Dutch heritage and wished I had a clearer identity and ethnicity, a place, a church, an origin, some roots. But to principal Bagoye and her teachers and students, I must have been from the same tribe as everyone else in our group: the Americans. The Californians. The surfers. In California as in Arusha, ethnicities and regional identities, like species, are becoming extinct every day.

After the games, the students joined together in long lines and mouthed the national anthem as we all sang together. Our students looked captivated and reverent as the whole Olastiti secondary school student body bid them goodbye. A student delegate stood before us and announced in her third language, "Thank you for visiting us, you are almost welcome." Principal Bagoye added in her fourth language, "Thank you all for choosing us among those special schools you visit. You are mostly welcome." Then, grinning and grateful, we set out on foot, waving goodbye to the rows of lucky students gathered around the Tanzanian flag at their new, local village school.

Skinning a goat with the Maasai (This was not the lesson I had planned).

Karibuni Stories
Blessing the Goat

**How much will we risk just to seize a "teachable moment"
that life serves up?**

As teachers, we're not paid to push limits - much. We plan lessons, most typically knowing what end is in store and what's on the test. We convince ourselves that many students need a reliable formula for successful learning, and that it is up to us to explain to them what's important. Safe in our classroom, we leave out mystery preferring to seek the known, which is strange if you explore the meanings of words like "teacher" and "education." But one day on the edge of the Serengeti Plains, we ended up out of bounds, out of that safety zone, and, for a while there, we did not know how to get back in.

As the day started out, a Maasai herdsman and cattle whistler named Barradit, spear in hand, walked us through the forest to a Wi-Fi hotspot. (You've never heard anyone whistle like Barradit.) I dispatched all this description as an email report to the parents back home, and loaded a whistling tune I learned from Barradit onto my smartphone so I could bring it home, just in case we needed any cattle called back in Southern California.

Presently, Barradit led us to the Land Rovers waiting for us and we motored out of Arusha in a bit of a trance.

After a while, the asphalt roads gave way to red clay in decent shape and corrugated aluminum roofs gave way to thatch as we began crossing the dry savannah, passing the Maasai herders dressed in their red or red and black three-piece togas, tending to their goats or cattle. We drove further across the dry plains of Maasailand of sprouting, spreading acacias, ancient, giant upside-down baobab trees, and dried out grazing lands with occasional dry soda ponds. It was September when the tsetse fly and mosquito populations are low and the usual, slightly overcast day was cool.

Our students gazed out the windows as the countryside passed them by. It was early in the trip and they were still mostly splintered into sleepy little duos and trios, still not a real team. Often, before a transformation like that happens and people really function and feel like a team, everyone has to overcome a significant, shared challenge or fear. They have to go through something real together.

It was a bumpy two hours until we arrived at our campsite in the mountains. The Maasai guides were busy setting up a cooking area near a tall slanted rock. There, roped to the makeshift kitchen, was a goat. This could only mean one thing. "I'd like to help with the slaughter," I told Killerai, our guide.

"Why do you want to do that?" he asked with his big smile, curious.

"Because I eat."

"Of course, you may slaughter the goat," he said. "I will tell the Maasai."

I assumed the students would be preoccupied setting

up their tents, scrambling on the rocks, napping, maybe even discovering a world without Facebook, and they would not notice any of the cooking activities. I don't know how word got out, but within a few minutes of my offer, the students were approaching me or the guides expressing either desire to help in the slaughter or anxiety that something like this could actually be happening. Their teacher was going to kill a wild creature and we would all eat it.

"To see things in their true proportion, to escape the magnifying influence of a morbid imagination, should be one of the chief aims of life," said William Edward Hartpole Lecky, in *The Map of Life*. Lecky's bronze statue stands before Trinity College in Dublin and yet I have to wonder if he ever worked with teens.

There was no escape now; it was time to tackle "morbid imagination" head on. No matter that this was a basic part of tribal life, Maddie, a senior who had just spent the summer rescuing wolves in Colorado, was inconsolable. Had I created a trauma?

Moments later, we gathered the students all together before a glowing Oldonyo Sambu sunset and formed a circle solemnly. One of our chaperones, Julie Chippendale, a nurse and yoga instructor, recited a Sufi prayer on all of life returning. Let us "pay the debt of our existence," she said.

Some others weighed in on the nature of sacrifice and the appreciation of the meat we eat. That the taking of the goat would be a blessing, life affirming. "I'll help, too," one student said, though it was not Maddie. "I want to watch," another added. One by one the students and teachers determined their relationship to the event and, in the end, all but two or three wanted to either watch or participate in the slaughter.

The time came. A Maasai wearing dusty chinos, sandals, and a black tee shirt with the word "Australia" printed across the front led the innocent goat out on a hemp rope. We gathered on a granite outcropping overlooking the valley below for a lesson about life in a vanishing Africa, beyond the veneer of textbooks and lectures. "Here, you may suffocate the goat," a Maasai offered to me, as another Maasai held the animal's legs back against a rock.

I resisted, "Not in front of all these students. When I offered, I didn't know everyone would watch." I was starting to think that maybe the students should leave. Was this a grave error? Even if not, could the parents back home ever understand? Amelia, an eighth grader and the youngest as well as one of the most articulate among us said, "We eat meat, and we need to learn..." and of course she was correct. I looked across the row of student eyes encircling the goat. Brandon looked scientific and matter of fact. Natalie looked inspired, but she always looked that way. Ahmad looked enthused, hungry—too much so, like many teenage boys.

"This is going to be phone calls when I get home," I said to the teacher standing next to me, as the Maasai guide firmly grasped and held the nose of the goat with a thick cloth. Amelia turned her head away, and the goat's wriggling slowly ceased.

The guides then began pulling the lifeless body taut as a Maasai worked his knife blade to separate various parts of meat. Amelia peeked a couple of times, then gradually drew her eyes in with everyone else's. Two other students were about ten feet away, peering out from behind a tree. As a teacher, it is a rare treasure to get in situations where everyone's instincts are all weighing in the same, where the line between teacher and student gets blurred and even disappears. At dusk now, the few clouds in the sky appeared to be turning from gold, to red, to grey.

The Maasai were clearly happy we had made possible the purchase of this life-giving goat. Never would we have fresher, more local, more organic meat. They continued carving masterfully, and everyone looked on in reverence and curiosity. This did not seem at all like a biology class dissection. "Not a drop of blood," Ahmad noted admiringly. I thought to myself that our students might either never eat meat again, or they would love it even more.

Next came the kidney, which the Maasai nibbled on a bit, and then passed around. Some of our students nibbled at it too and felt the squish of the fresh organ. "It's like lychee," someone says. And then a blue plastic bowl filled with precious goat blood was circulating. To the Maasai this is the healthiest part of all.

"This is phone calls," I moaned to somebody, wiping the blood from my fingers. But of course it was too late. My only choice was to trust our students. Now the carver began separating the useful skin, as a Maasai walked away with a bucket of meat parts to hang on a row of wooden spits above the bonfire.

Gradually the African sky grew inky black and we gathered around the campfire. After a while, the meat was cooked, turning from red to brown. The smell was savory. We moved in closer around the campfire, all eighteen of us. You can always witness a diverse group starting to come together when circles start to form. Normally we find a symbolic object to place in the center of our circles, but this time we had a real center. Meat. Things that had been mysteries were now seemingly normal. Up above, Scorpio had appeared. Thor, a ninth grade student, said, "At home, I'm a vegetarian, but here, this is good." The meat was pretty tough but, out here as a tribe, who cared? It just meant you savored it longer.

After finishing our plates, the Maasai formed a group in front of us and did a dance impersonating a hyena, elephant and lion, their spears moving up and down as they chanted. Wild orange flames from the campfire illuminated their flowing, red Shúkà and faces. And at last, as a school, we were all one. Unity.

This was not the lesson I had planned. After a while, we yawned and people drifted off to the tents. One Maasai stood out all night with his spear, the long, bladed side facing upwards to fend off lions.

In a Botswana Orphanage (with Botswanan haircut):
What do we have to offer?

Karibuni Stories
How Do You Educate a Warrior?
(Emboreet)

How do you educate a warrior? Are warrior qualities relevant to schooling?

When we first saw a woman wrapped in brightly colored robes moving gracefully down the side of the dirt road with a bucket on her head as we travelled through eastern Tanzania deep into Maasailand, I nearly jumped out of my seat to capture an image of her soul inside my camera. Each step she took was so dignified, so epochal, as though the whole Earth and its history were her balance beam. My pulse quickened and I snapped the shutter before it was too late.

We pressed on through Tanangire National Park, past a lioness guarding a half-finished wildebeest carcass. Then dropped gradually down towards the Great Rift Valley where we camped on the Southwest side of the park. The next day, we continued heading east through dry plains on which we spotted wandering herdsmen with goats, donkeys and cattle. Ostriches. There were termite mounds three times the height of a zebra. And the occasional baobab tree; wide-spreading flame trees that transfixed our eyes. We passed through tiny villages with mud huts.

Pressing on deeper into the country, at last, we reached the dry, wide-open plain called Emboreet and far down barely discernable dirt paths, at last, The Emboreet School.

"Knowledge is like a garden; if it is not cultivated, it cannot be harvested," goes the African proverb. But there were no gardens out here. Emboreet is an expanse of pastoralists living, at least to a fair extent, as they have for centuries. And risks like human and cattle disease and drought were only just starting to be viewed as things you can actually do something about, beyond migrating. It can take a twelve-hour day or a thirty-kilometer round trip walk to get water, which keeps many Maasai nomadic. Some of the children walk half that far for a day at Emboreet School, rather than tending their herds.

Out here, elementary classes can have up to 70 students in them. The state Ministry of Education supplies the curriculum. It is the same one they supply for schools in Dar es Salaam, a crowded coastal city and commerce center where there are no herds or baobab trees. As a community educator, I was wondering: What is an Emboreet education? Will there be anything in this community that local schooling can sustain rather than being replaced with whatever the state serves up? Will the local Maasai traditions play a part?

We pulled in to the schoolyard and were greeted by the officials and some Maasai elders who had come around to see visitors from afar. They were tall and dignified looking in their robes. One had a black wool ski cap with the word "Obama" scrolling across the front. Did he know the re-election campaign was underway? There was an L-shaped building of eight classrooms with rusting corrugated aluminum roofing, enfolding a red-clay plot punctuated with dry, wispy trees, and a couple of matching dorms which did not look well populated. Two donkeys lolled around. Two water cisterns dotted a perimeter of scrub and succulents, but not much laid beyond that. These were the last vestiges of the traditional, nomadic community.

The Maasai children bunched together to greet us, rather than line up like the kids did in the schools that are close to the city. About half were in their uniforms of yellow tee-shirt tops and green skirts or shorts, colors from the Tanzanian flag. They sang a welcoming song. It was in English and was so rhythmic that soon we were all involuntarily bobbing our heads:

> We welcome you, to our school,
> (louder) We welcome you, to our school.
> Clap-Clap, clap clap clap clap,
> Clap-Clap, clap clap clap clap.
> We welcome you-oo, to our schoo-ool,
> We welcome you-oo, to our schoo-ool.
> Na nana nan-nan-nan, clap clap clap,
> Na nana nan-nan-nan, clap clap clap.

Charlie, one of our high school freshmen, had been traveling all week with a thick paperback on the political history of Tanzania. He had also been studying Swahili and read a welcoming script he had composed. The Maasai students listened with a mix of fascination and disbelief, clapping at every pause. Though they had nothing prepared, I coaxed two of our student musicians into singing a song for the children. After all, the children had sung for us. Thor accompanied Natalie on ukulele as they performed a very hip, alternative music song by a band called *Of Monsters and Men*, a song not made for clapping along with, while the little Maasai gathered before us looking on, concerned: if you can't clap or sing along with music, what are you supposed to do?

A few Maasai young teens looked on from the outskirts of the school compound, arms folded, hovering. For the most part, teens seeking schooling would have to go to a boarding facility in the city; that is, if they could pay the fees. That could cost around $1000 a year for families used to living on a dollar or two a day. The locals of Emboreet hoped that someday this school would board four or five hundred secondary students. At least that was the original plan. The other plan, only in whispers, involved gigantic Chinese crews plowing highways through this area as the locals were displaced.

We talked with the principal awhile and explained we had arts and sports stuff for them and would enjoy playing with the kids. They were excited to get started as we broke off into a couple of classrooms. With walls of dull yellow and powder blue, a smudged blackboard and rows of bench desks, these could have been classrooms in any country.

School hopping, we always find student interaction in the elementary classroom to be very different than in the high school classroom. Here in an elementary classroom, there could be no discussion forum. Yet with almost no common language, conditions were perfect for sharing art. We gave out a pencil and two or three crayons to everyone we could so that we could begin drawing, and each of our students got a group of two or more elementary students. The Maasai kids were almost overwhelmed at this way of organizing. How many tourists ask to spend the day with them at their school? They were incredibly joyful and filled with smiles. The melodic banter of Maasai and Swahili filled the room.

An older child was so overenthusiastic he tried to take a pencil from a little one, and one of our students sorted that out. Paper was unbelievably scarce in this school, so we took the 8 ½ by 11 sheets we had brought and carefully tore them into fours. Now there was almost enough to go around, if we used both sides.

As overwhelming as all the paper and drawing materials were, more overwhelming to the children was the presence of a dozen, smiling, light-skinned teens from a faraway land, all wanting to draw and sing with them. They physically attached to our students, hugging and hanging on to every word, grinning and giggling politely, absorbed in drawing beautiful pictures of Serengeti wildlife, bomas (homesteads), beautiful images of birds, tribesmen, fish and flowers. Lots of flowers. We all drew until there was no more paper.

Gradually, other Maasai students were coming outside where we had brought not only soccer balls, but air pumps, too. There was no groundcover, but the sandy red clay yard was smooth enough to play the French Open. And globally, soccer balls never fail. Soccer stimulates self-organization and collaboration amongst any diverse group. We have even done this with Israeli and Arab ethnicities. Soccer is language. We had more Frisbees, too. By the slight shade of a dry thorn tree, a group of seven huddled in with fascination as they passed around Thor's ukulele. We played like this for an hour and it felt as though we had spread goodwill. But we had many miles to cover and, since it was not a regular school day, these students may have had goats and cattle to herd.

We loaded into the Land Rovers and one of the herdsman who was at the school directed us to his homestead, his boma, a rare glimpse of another world. In the country, the Maasai herdsmen live with the goats, cattle and two or three wives to tend them.

Once inside his boma, we walked over to a hut surrounded by baby goats and then into its open doorway. There we found an entry wall with a sign reading: "Karibuni WA WA." "Welcome people." Unexpectedly, the herdsman invited us to enter the hut. We ambled in, ducking into the main, round room with its two tiny, low sleeping alcoves. It was dark and we were met first by two eyes, set back in a corner. Wife number one. We moved quietly like trespassers.

Outside again, we walked in front of another hut where there was another wife with her bald, rheumy-eyed mother. Along with some chickens and dogs, her three little boys in patchwork robes and ear piercings hovered around holding their wooden cattle prods. We had not seen them in the school that day. We all glanced about and scoped out the topography, this life, their every day. Behind the boma, the prairie ran as far as the eye could see.

There is limited secondary school in Emboreet. Girls marry at between ages 12 and 18, sometimes as arranged around the time of their birth if someone has paid an agreed-upon price. The lives of these girl and women are on the boma, where they gather firewood, carry water (unless they have a donkey), build the houses, cook, and milk the cows.

All this may change though if the Maasai are coerced into moving by the government to areas where they can farm reliably. And, as hard as their life seems, if the past 10,000 years is any indication, loss of the herder lifestyle and transition into a farming life will make things a whole lot harder. The point of the government push is that herders and hunters make it difficult for officials to carve up the land into taxable chunks whereas farmland is easy to levy taxes against. This is no world for a Maasai warrior.

Of course, education is changing a lot of this. NGOs are paying for more of the girls to go to boarding schools. But is this an advance toward a better life? The Maasai love their native language. Will it die out? Will the development of all these schools across the plains put these children into a low-end mimicry of Western schooling, six-hour days of restrictions and artificial book learning preparing them for ... what? For over a century now, people have been speculating on when the Maasai will cease to exist. Is this mandatory national schooling standard going to help bring about their demise?

I shot photographs of the faces and already knew that they were hopelessly too good, here now, but vanishing. This life is all too precious; its time is running out. We said our goodbyes, and continued heading east through dry, red, reedy plains. We passed two women—grain they had milled and bagged is strapped to the side of a donkey on their way to a market somewhere, something we would not have seen a decade ago. Are they walking into the Maasai future?

Eventually we began ascending, winding up a red, clay road and up the Rift Escarpment to the congested town of Mulu where electrical wires crisscross overhead, where giraffe meat is supposedly labeled as "beef," and Pepsis are sold on every corner but only shillings are taken for them, no dollars. We continued climbing up toward dusty plains with young cow herders and their siblings, just happy children, herding, walking along the way. We were headed across the Great Rift Valley, deeper into the bush still farther from civilization. We were out of paper and soccer balls. What did we have to offer now?

Hadza children learn by mimicry. Here: arrow-making.

"Long ago...
No one tore the ground with ploughshares
or parceled out the land
or swept the sea with dipping oars —
the shore was the world's end.
Clever human nature, victim of your intentions,
disastrously creative,
why cordon cities with towered walls?
Why arm for war?"

—Ovid

Karibuni Stories

Unschooling

Where do students learn more at school, in or out of class?
Is the role of the teacher to liberate or control students?

Our guide, Killerai, was dusting off the Land Rover. We had driven southwest, several hours from Arusha, Tanzania, through tribal lands and villages with smiling children waving along the side of the road, past cattle prodded along by little boys with sticks, across river valleys, and were now preparing to go switch-backing down into the Great Rift Valley and across it.

The Great Rift Valley is a crack in the Earth running six-thousand miles from around the Dead Sea, all the way down to Kenya in the south of Africa. It is the only landform you can see from the moon. We were going to cross over it, the world on the other side being unlike anything we'd ever seen or are likely to see again.

The valley is a flat salt pan that was dry enough

around that time of year, September, to drive across, and even then only if you could avoid cracks in the Earth and the occasional mud sink. With two vehicles filled with students rapidly dehydrating, I was shaking my head once again, fretting, "This time I'm definitely gonna get parent phone calls."

By the time we reached the other side, we could sense the Great Rift had cut us off from a familiar Africa. The Rover began climbing the far side of the Escarpment, steep and rocky, passing small grass huts and dry scrub. People moving very slowly with long, rough wooden spears signaled a different realm. We were in one of the last, inhabited parts of the natural world, the tribal land of the Hadza.

Daudi Peterson re-discovered these people around 40 years prior to our visit. A Dutch missionary who had just finished his post, he determined to make contact with the tribe and so, driving far out into their lands, filled an oil drum with tobacco and lit it. The people came from miles around at the rich smell of their only luxury. That was the start of the Dorobo Guides.

The Hadza are believed to be one of the only remaining hunter-gatherer societies in the world. There are probably about 700 Hadzape remaining of a 40,000-year heritage in the area. They do not herd cattle. They do not grow crops. If they are not hungry enough to eat whatever food they find today, then they won't remove it from the Earth. As such, study of the past or future is of minimal importance in Hadza education. They would be puzzled if not amused by our educational obsession with the prefrontal lobe, always planning for predictable outcomes. On the other hand, people all over my town in Southern California talk often of living life "in the present moment," and at this, the Hadza are clearly at guru level.

We pulled into a heavily wooded clearing where the Hadza had already set up the mess tent for us. They were dressed in hand-me-downs, animal skins, and colorful beadwork. Hence, the Hadza lifestyle is similar to the way it's been for hundreds of years, maybe thousands. Soon after our arrival we followed the men and women into the woods, as it was time to gather tuber roots for food. This we did successfully with our digging sticks. A small child always seemed to be toddling around, punching his little digging stick here and there. We felt responsible to observe but not influence, as though we were in a museum.

Way back when the missionaries came and left *Bibles*, the Hadza used the pages to roll and smoke tobacco. They seem impervious to the western and increasingly global illusion that we can and should make life whatever we want it to be. The Hadza have fended off such influences with incredible tenacity and consistency. What's more, their children receive no education. At no time does a Hadza parent tell the child what to do, nor did they tell us what to do. This creates a paradox for us but is the most natural thing in the world to them; they pass along their culture primarily by not schooling.

Such concepts, occasionally called "unschooling," where students pursue their own inclinations freely and with trust, are well known to Western educators and psychologists, and supportive research is easy to find, even if it is widely ignored in practice. For instance, as Deci concluded, "In terms of education, it has become ever more apparent that self-determination, in the forms of intrinsic motivation and autonomous internalization, leads to the types of outcomes that are beneficial both to individuals and to society." In fact, there are hundreds of "free schools" in the United States and thousands worldwide, a whisper of a movement whose time will surely come.

Anthropologists have noted that the Hadza do not beat or scold their children, as they must presume that the child's instinct is the main thing worthy of their trust. The child's educational guide is their own free will, as nature has designed it. Developmental psychologist Peter Grey details this, citing research from anthropologists who have observed Hadza and other scarce and threatened hunter-gatherer tribes, "They run, chase, leap, climb, throw, and dance, and in doing so they develop fit and coordinated bodies. They make musical instruments and play the familiar ...songs and create new ones. They do all this because they want to. Nobody tells them they must. Nobody tests them."

World over, most schooling emphasizes accountability, meaning that the will and free spirit of a fair number of our youth are drummed out of them over years of mandatory sitting in rows for hours every day and ranking the value of each based fundamentally upon how compliant they are with our requirements and standards. Hadza children are subject to no such competitions or judgments. They merely play. Through mimicry of their elders, they care for infants, build huts and tools, make fires, defend against make-believe predators, and tell stories. If their parents have quarreled, they may rehash it the next day in playful mimicry. Suicide and anxiety are incomprehensible. They learn to stay alive and healthy naturally.

Out in a field our first morning with these children, they found us honeycomb high up in some tree branches, the sweetest treat I have ever tasted. They also made miniature bows and arrows for fun, and we saw eight or nine year-olds who appeared to be stalking small creatures. Our Southern California students tried their hand at all this. It struck them as a nice life.

Some Hadza leave the tribe forever. Some try their hand at city jobs for a while and then return to the tribe and its simpler ways. Why not quit your job as an urban trash collector and return to the land for a two to three hour workday? Primarily, though, as Peter Matthiessen put it, the Hadza "ask nothing from the rest of us but to be left alone."

As with the neighboring Maasai tribe, the Tanzanian government tried for many years to pressure or entice the Hadza to turn to an agrarian lifestyle, as does the occasional church or do-gooder service group. But they have continued to resist. Farming would be too much work. Moreover, their simple, sustainable ways would have been lost forever. On October 18, 2011, the Hadza living in the Yaeda valley were at last issued deeds for land encompassing more than 20,000 hectares of land. A culmination of years of strategy and work, this was a momentous occasion and a historical precedent in Tanzania. The Hadza can now be left alone.

The Hadza elders treated us as they treat their own children, which is to say, with enormous respect. We found them to be uniformly good-natured and free of apparent burden as they lived in the balance of nature in ways we might find isolating and arduous back home. We found no age divisions or groupings as Hadza children played. Younger children learn from older, sometimes in great fun. If any of our group or any small child sat down next to an elder or grandparent who was beading or arrow-making and showed curiosity, we would see the elder slow down and begin to share this activity gladly, guiding our less experienced hands.

One morning, we helped manufacture arrows, sliding smooth sticks across the fire, then bending any kinks out of the wood with our teeth. That afternoon, we all set off to go hunting. My group was lead by an elder, Kou'unda. He carried a baboon fur-trimmed bow strung with giraffe tendon.

We walked a few miles on foot as the rough, wagon-style track gave way to single, red clay trails. We followed closely, through the woods and meadows, as Kou'unda peeked around corners, listening for signs of game. But nothing. We said little because we had yet to discover any common words.

At a rest stop, by a cave, he showed the students a little known "click" word, which is made by popping the tongue off the roof of the mouth. "Click-baago." It means, arrow. "Click-baago," he said again. He somehow gestured to make me understand that he liked my hiking boots and wanted them. I didn't know why, because his feet looked completely adapted to the local terrain. I wondered too if perhaps we had no business introducing foreign objects into this indigenous situation. I replied, "Hiking boots." He smiled.

We climbed a rise into a heavily shaded area surrounded with six-foot rock outcroppings when Kou'unda suddenly turned on his heel, looked at us, put his finger to his mouth, a universal sign I guess, and we stopped in our tracks while he slid an arrow into his bow. Kou'unda had heard something. A second later, we too heard a soft drumming. Kou'unda crouched. Then, "tap," hooves on rock, and our hearts pounded. A blur of something like a small deer bounded up, lightly touched his forepaws on the rock for added thrust, then leapt overhead while Kou'unda wheeled around and let go a poison-tipped arrow. Before we could think this blur had disappeared into the thick woods.

A klipspringer. Kou'unda walked over to the rocks and fished around some, then came walking back with two broken objects from an arrow: the decapitated top and the feathered bottom. He pointed to the front of the arrow and said, looking down, "click-baago." The valuable arrowhead was gone. Crestfallen or reflective, I couldn't tell which, he extracted a cigarette rolling paper out of his pants pocket with a pinch of tobacco and rolled one up. Then he drew his hunting knife from out of its sheath, sliced a small branch off a tree, and fashioned a four-inch platform into which he hollowed out a small bowl with the tip of his knife. He then rounded off the edges of his broken arrow, carefully letting the shavings fall into the tiny tinder bowl. I took a second to savor the timelessness of this moment, especially for my students.

I've travelled and studied with outdoorsmen and survivalists, including Native Americans, all over the United States but had never seen anything like this. In close to two minutes he had constructed both an ancient-style bow drill and a cigarette, created fire, and now sat in the shade, plaintively smoking. That klipspringer would have been a week's worth of meat.

When he was done smoking, I searched into his dark eyes looking for words, and found, very slowly: "Kou'unda, I'm sorry. I'm sorry." This was so different than the things I was normally sorry about. I had to wonder if the Hadza had a better word. In turn, he took off his own bracelet, fit it onto my wrist. "My friend," he said in English. "My friend."

I unbuttoned the beaded wrist bracelet I'd bought in the market, and offered it up in return. He looked at the bracelet and said only, "Maasai," took it from my hand with a nod, and put it on.

Walking back, from behind, I studied Kou'unda's gait carefully. He never once even broke a twig passing through the brush—I don't know how he did that. It reminded me that sensitivity to the environment is the truest meaning of intelligence that I knew, something his children would surely learn. His feet tracked in a single line, and we mimicked in single file, as good students.

It is an ancient and still contemporary precept that two ideas can contradict each other and also be true. Few spaces on Earth remain outside the reach of national bureaucracies seeking compulsory, standardized education in the name of "unity" or "equity." And yet, the more education we force on our children, the less time, space and freedom there is for their own, intimate searches for meaning. Most of our educational heroes have said no less, whether we look to Dewey, Fröbel, Einstein,

Montessori, Piaget or even Socrates, who willingly drank hemlock and died in defense of this idea.

In the five years prior to our visit to Tanzania, 1500 community schools were built across Tanzania, all with an eye towards delivering a more accessible, more uniform, state-approved education to the youth across the country. It is perfectly within the realm of imagination that all this public work to further transform a land into a nation could invite both the greatest liberation and the greatest educational loss of the new millennium. What great unity awaits the future of students and tribes? What vast and timeless spirit will be gone? Because for some of the tribes, the federal pursuit of equity will mean the extinction of their identity *and* ethnicity.

On our last night with the Hadza, we cooked our catch—a tortoise and an irax—on the rocks of the campfire. (A year or so later we read in *National Geographic* that tortoise was the original "paleo-diet.") Our native teachers sang songs all evening to the melodies of the handmade, two-string, gourd zither, and they sounded strikingly like traditional Appalachian fiddle tunes. I had one translated:

> A man has such trouble.
> Won't you help?
> He has leprosy.
> Help him.
> He has misery.

These lyrics were maybe a thousand years old. Perhaps even older. Ballads like this hold lessons that transcend time and human culture. They convey the universal sense of loneliness. Pain. Loss. Are we supposed to fix this? I looked around at my twelve students gathered around the circle and I wished ballads for them. I wished we could convey ballads that transcended the artificiality of first world matters back home.

The next morning, we loaded the Rovers and headed back to the city for our long journey home, first stopping at the Hadza settlement at the foot of the hill to say goodbye. There, men and boys hovered around just being while the village mothers sat beading, their small ones close at hand, all circled around a spreading acacia tree. Now, a year later, the bracelet Kou'unda gave me is still on my wrist.

Lakota and California kids hacky sacking under the Wounded Knee Cemetery gateway.

> *"Your inside is out and your outside is in."*
> —John Lennon & Paul McCartney

A Gateway

What does it mean to have "open space" in school or classroom? What are the factors that make a class or campus high trust and low threat?

Through the looking glass, into the woods, across the bridge . . . literature and the arts are filled with gateways and portals. "There is always one moment in childhood when the door opens and lets the future in," Graham Greene intuits as we hope every parent and teacher will. Spanish mythology describes the *duende*, that special place or gateway zone and we cannot even know if it is all around us or deep inside us. Or both. It is the zone Socrates was in when he drank the hemlock, or perhaps just the walk we take home once school is out of the summer and we are ten years old. Once, up on the Pine Ridge Indian Reservation, one student group had a moment like this, a door-opening moment.

It was not a big deal or even a whole story, it was only a moment, but I think about that moment often when I enter a school. After visiting with some Lakota friends from Red Cloud Indian School, some Southern California students and teachers from The Grauer School were headed east on Route 18 South Dakota, then turned left on Big Foot Trail and headed north a while. They approached a small knoll you could almost miss if you did not feel the gravity of it, and parked. There, they ambled up the stubby grass and stony dirt to the legendary site of one of the worst days in American history. There was no one around.

Towards the top were two gateposts, five paces apart, made of white painted cinderblocks and plain red bricks. These were bridged on top by an arch of welded, crisscrossed bars. Next to it, a piece of scrap plywood with a spray painted arrow and the words "THE WOUNED KNEE MUSEUM" across it was tied to the chain link fence. At the foot of the hill, a family was flying an American flag upside down.

The students passed through the archway, entering the small graveyard. For the site of something so monumental in the history of a whole race of people, there wasn't much around. Mostly just big, empty prairies in all directions. They wandered about, reflecting on the graves and reading tombstones. On the perimeter of the yard, underneath a lone, young pine, was the wooden cross of Marvin M. Two Two. The marker, colorfully painted with native-style designs, showed he had died in 1993. They paid respects.

In the middle of the site was the 1903 granite monument listing many who were lost at the massacre and buried in the mass grave. Some of the students kneeled down and lit some sage in honor of those lost, in honor of those people who made peace with the infinite, or maybe in honor of the whole lost world. "Mitakuye Oyasin," we all said, *mitok-wee-ossin*, passing the sage around, though our imaginations, however sincere or vivid, could never grasp the horror of what had really happened here.

Two students had wandered off, and were under the

gateway. The two were Keanan and Thor, both in baggy shirts, baggy pants and sneakers kicking a hacky sack. Forming a circle with them were two native Lakota kids who had appeared in baggy pants, baggy shirts and sneakers. They were engrossed in the game, kicking the little foot bag around, but unlike most games we have with kids we meet on the road, there were no teams. They hardly said a word, and all eight eyes transfixed the little, cloth ball as it arched and hung in the air after each kick, timeless little moments of perfection.

Les Hart coined the word "downshifting" to describe the behavior of the mind if some violation of territoriality is deeply felt. When we perceive threat, things appear more starkly black and white to us, our minds are more rigid, and we divide the world into insiders versus outsiders.

But there was none of that under the gateway; no downshifting, no outsiders, no genders or tribes. "The *duende* . . . where is the *duende*?" the Poet Garcia Lorca wrote. "Through the empty archway a wind of the spirit enters, blowing insistently over the heads of the dead, in search of new landscapes and unknown accents: a wind with the odour of a child's spit, crushed grass, and Medusa's veil, announcing the endless baptism of freshly created things." There is a power and knowing such as the *duende* described in every culture, even a reliance upon it, except perhaps in our modern culture which has withdrawn from it, banished miracles, hacked away all but our five, measurable senses, and replaced so much of this magic knowing with fear and exhaustion. There in the gateway our kids were taking that quality back for a moment there, a moment for all time, trading places, moving about, just keeping the hacky sack in the air.

That was it. Like I said, it was not a whole story, just an image, though more than an image it was a transition frozen in time.

Children are natural lovers of magic, yearning for "what lies beyond," and yet, through years of schooling we can see this sense erode along with the courage and patience to seek it out. What a blissful moment it was, up on the Pine Ridge Indian Reservation, one of the most troubled places in the nation, to see students creating a permeable gateway, an open space. Any school could use a tolerance gateway like this, where things are beyond language and would not have to be either true or not true. Where the ball's up in the air and it can't ever touch the ground.

Children's art from Palestine: hearts and guns.

*"If you are involved with the intensity of crescendo situations,
with the intensity of tragedy, you might begin to see
the humor of these situations as well."*

—Chögyam Trungpa Rinpoche

Samaya
Parent and the Teacher

**What is the "barrier" between parents and teachers in
schools? What would happen if it went away?**

On June 24, 2013, 5:34 PM, Stuart Grauer emails:
"I'm free Friday AM for some mellow
stand-up paddle surf if you can get free."

Later:

On June 24, 2013, 7:29 PM, Thomas Chippendale
writes back:

"I would like that. It is a bit crazy now with
appointments and decisions."

Then a week later, on June 31, 2013, 7:16 AM:

"Ok, Stuart, if the surf is not huge, we are on!!
(I heard there was a swell coming.) It is in my
calendar! —Tom"

I picked Tom up at nine and he said, "We can't go for
the long paddle down the bluffs of Torrey Pines. I have to
be back at the hospital by eleven." I didn't know if it was
his job or his treatment he needed to be there for. Anyway,

I got the idea he was tentative and might slide out of this whole thing if he had an excuse, although I guess he did. We loaded up the boards on top of my Ford wagon and stowed the paddles.

We arrived at Cardiff Reef at 9:15 and it looked solid, chest high, with whitewater streaming in strong. So it was not going to be an easy, mellow paddle out. We'd probably be hit a few times. Tom remained tentative. His leg hurt more than he thought it would and he explained that if he stood up wrong and strained himself it could send a third blood clot into his brain. He already had two.

Tom's daughter, Jayne, had graduated from our school eight years earlier so he and I had her as a permanent connection between us. In small schools, where there is not much bureaucracy separating those we work with and work for, this happens a lot—though it occurs gradually over time. I hadn't noticed Tom much while Jayne was a student. But it was easy to notice her, a starry-eyed jewel with innocence like water, so pure, so clear. It made me wonder if, as teachers, all we could do is pollute waters like these, and I still wonder about this.

Tom, a neurologist, in those days seemed a little preoccupied and intellectual, like he was tapped into some reverent source. He always wore one of those warm, knowing smiles. There on the other side of his glasses was a deep calm, and I suspect that was the calm universal consciousness he referred to often in his teachings as "the netherworld between the mind and the brain," as though his prefrontal cortex reached deep down to his pineal gland. Quiet. Rooted. Connected.

Suddenly, facing the ocean breaking hard and cold,

the groundlessness of all life, how incredibly unmapped our largest journey is, was filling in. It was like a little crack had opened and dark was slipping through, and then it closed up as we got our feet wet, but I knew it was always there. Strangely, fear felt inseparable from courage at that moment, and I sensed that Tom was somehow teaching me this. I just didn't know how. All I could say was, "You're my freakin' hero, Tom. Paddling out at the risk of a blood clot." I suggested that all we needed to do was paddle out, not go anywhere. Just to get out there past the break would be a victory, even if we didn't ride waves. I didn't know if he bought it.

Tom paddled half way out, almost through the whitewater when a set approached. I thought, "Trouble." A wave welled up and tumbled him as I watched in terror but he just scrambled back on the board and started paddling again, cautious, but resolute to get out of the impact zone. At last, past the break, we stood up on our boards and began our paddling, heading north towards the bluffs of Encinitas. By the time we reached the break called Tippers, Tom was obviously tired so we paddled just a bit further. He sat down on his board, looked in towards the shore, and said, "This is where Julie and I come."

Since that day, every time I paddle past that spot, just north of Cardiff Reef and Tippers, I always think, "Tom and Julie's."

So, we sat and rested at Tom and Julie's, Tom doing nothing, sort of gathering himself. Jerry Granelli, the jazz musician, once said, "Just being with your fear, just being with it, is the most powerful form of fearlessness." Maybe that is what was happening. He sat up squarely and rested.

Next, he stood up on the board and paddled, looking for a wave, and presently an outsider came, then picked up. He was paddling as it was lifting. It was going to be a late takeoff. He paddled a couple of times on the face as it crested but it pitched forward and he tumbled straight down into the trough of the wave and it swallowed him whole. I held my breath a little in suspense and paddled closer, but up he popped, grasping the board, and pulled himself back up. I don't know why, but I laughed. He grinned, and nodded.

So he sat for a while, catching his breath and taking five. He had his head down a bit, like he was listening to what was emerging from himself, irretrievably committed to something. There was something compelling about his expression as he rested there, not his usual soft smile, and I've often wondered what was going on in his mind over those moments. Maybe he was thinking how crazy it was that out here, in the vastness of the ocean and sky, that we could think a surfboard is something we can really grasp, that there might be anything for us to hold on to. Maybe he was turning daggers into flowers. Maybe he was just clearing his mind. Or maybe his gaze looked so compelling because he didn't have his glasses on.

He stood himself up again and we paddled around, trying once more to stalk a wave, searching the outside lineup, until he said, "I haven't even got a wave yet." I answered, "Hey, why don't we just paddle back and head in, you already took the biggest drop of the day. That was an awesome drop." But he paddled in closer to the break zone and said, "I haven't had a wave." I was wondering if he was wondering what I was wondering: will this be the last wave of his life? We jockeyed around for wave position and, next thing, this nice three footer approached. He paddled, it picked him up and he was streaming out in front of it, then carving right as the wave carried him down the line, then re-formed half way in. He glided across the inside section, synchronously, heading towards the lagoon mouth and all the way to the sand for the longest ride of the day. Victory. I caught the next wave in and we were done.

"That gave me courage," he said, laying his board down on the sand.

I went to pull the car around to where our boards were, then pulled out a mini bottle of tequila, saying with a little grin, "You don't have to do this." He said, "Yea, I probably shouldn't."

I took out two shot glasses, poured a little for me, then a splash for him. I cut a couple of slices off a lime and stuck them in the glasses. I licked my wrist then sprinkled some coarse Israeli salt on it. "It goes like this. Cheers," I said, licking my salty wrist, throwing back the tequila which was unbelievably smooth and woody, then sticking the lime wedge in my mouth. And I held up the other glass and said, "Here, Tom, it's just a splash."

The situation before, sitting there outside the break, had left me feeling frozen when I examined myself inside and really imagined being in his shoes. But not Tom.

I don't think it's vulnerability or weakness that makes you vulnerable or weak. I think it's really just the fear of those things. I felt as though I had watched a man size all this up right before my eyes and move into the fearless zone. He knocked back his drink. "Tom, you went surfing knowing that it could send a clot to your brain, and you got the wave of the day. You're a freakin' animal. You're a warrior."

As we turned the corner out of the parking lot heading down the road for home, he said, "I'm going to be okay." Then he explained it all to me. All the craziness from a technical standpoint, but with so much care. He talked like I was the patient not him. Like you'd have to love this man as your doctor, as a healer. But, notwithstanding the explanations, I would have been terrified to be the patient so it had to be him. It was an undeniable thing that was emerging from inside him and within six months it would take his life.

We rounded a curve and a squirrel was curled up in a ball squirming in the middle of the road. Tom looked at me and said, like a scientist considering an experiment, "That was really smooth, where'd you get that tequila?" It was Herradura Anejo. Taking the bait, I said, "Pour a little shot." But he was concerned he had to get to the hospital, so I said, "Tom, take the shot, they'll love you. They'll ask why you don't come in mellow like this every day. Pour another shot, Tom." And he poured a splash. Cheers. We rounded the curve and Tom knocked it back. Liquid smoke.

Starting out as a young teacher, I of course could never have envisioned an ending like that: head of the local school with the chief of staff of the local hospital, cruising home from the surf, knocking it back, but there it was. "You're my freakin' hero," I said into the silence. "You really are."

Tom gave a half grin, a Buddha-grin, and looked

straight out down the road. That was some moment, incredibly not crazy. He nodded his head and said, "That's really smooth."

A Swiss girl from California connects with Navajo girl from New Mexico.
It is the presence of significant relationships that makes learning matter.

"Those who tell the stories, rule the people."
—Navajo proverb

Navajo School
(How Miracles Happen)

Is it the job of the school to pass along local and ethnic culture? What is the role of the school in the community?

O
ur visit to New Mexico took a quick turn when a teacher from the Navajo School called in sick. Rather than pay for a substitute teacher, the principal assigned us, a whole class of high school kids from Southern California, to be the subs. We began planning and plotting like mad, but were destined to find that hardly anything we could think of would end up working to engage the Navajo classes. Until, in the end, the most obvious thing in the world worked.

8:00 AM. The local kids entered the classroom, apparently overwhelmed with disenfranchisement and isolation. They flopped into their chairs in rows, and the unmistakable message based upon years of schooling was that they could only succeed by reading pages 82-89 and answering questions about French and Dutch explorers entering the Great Lakes region. And why would they want to do that? There was a listlessness in the atmosphere.

. . . Just down the road were canyons as magnificent as we could imagine—wind weaved through cottonwoods carrying ancient memories, songs, dances, spirit. These canyon walls breathed the story of conquistadors and escape. On another day, we would walk there with a Navajo guide who said, "My grandfather teaches that

all religions and paths are good if they help you walk in beauty." Our students naturally sought out our guide's calm, ancient wisdom as they followed him through rock formations and canyons they would never approach alone. Here was a real teacher. If only men like him could be in the schools, but there is no way a man like him would be. If only this was the school . . .

Back in the school itself was a sense of despair. This was not just any despair—it felt hopeless, intractable. The culture is obviously endangered, the language is "severely threatened," and the main concern of the school district is the standardized test scores and compliant behaviors of its students.

One Navajo teacher had explained there are few parents raising their own kids these days—it is the grandparents. A poster in the back of the room said, "There are a lot of cool things about being native, meth isn't one of them." The atmosphere felt scattered, the acoustics somehow disturbing.

We jumped into our plan. A circle! Some Grauer School students formed a large, standing circle, begging the local kids to get out of their chairs and join. A few dragged themselves into the circle, where they threw a ball around and introduced themselves and their interests. But there was little reason for connection. Everyone retreated to their desks.

The problems in the Navajo school appeared as unknowable as the empty faces of these students. In this middle school class, one student had been expelled five times. He had eleven siblings or step-siblings and his mother lived on another reservation. "I absolutely hate school, but it means I don't have to go home," he told Rory, a ninth grade Grauer School student. This reservation may be bounded by four sacred mountains, but it is still a place of dire poverty and disharmony.

Odds are, more than half of these students will not graduate high school. A teacher here does not last long either.

The students are lucky if a teacher finishes a single year. And so, the first period passed in inertness. In the absence of a teacher, we beach town, visiting substitute teachers regrouped and addressed our failure. Would the day pass like this?

Our students walked over to the Navajo kids in rows and tried to help, but few wanted it. There was nothing in this for them. "I have a zero point eight average," one student said with a little attitude. "I don't get to play in the football games, but the coach lets me go to the practices."

Class ended, another group of students padded in slowly with no affect. "It feels like prison," one of our students observed. Call it what you will. We were not allowed to take them outside.

We walked over to help one student or another and examined the assignment for this second class. In the textbook, as if by some trick of providence, the day's assignment entailed coverage of the Navajo people. It was September and this is a topic that came early in the history book. It was the section on Neolithic culture and we could see that the native people were treated as colorful, bygone relics rather than as the present-day vital source of culture and spirit they are to so many people we would meet all week long. Based on the textbook, not a whole lot had happened since First Man and First Woman planted corn.

"I hate history. I only care about the present," a student said. We thought, "Then what are you going to do right NOW?" but no one would say that because what he needed was not alien advice but understanding. And although we would spend some of the next week talking about what we should have said, the perfect comeback, at that moment, all anyone in the room could feel was a sense of despair. The co-teachers huddled up to talk strategy again.

We had had enough of the State curriculum. Clayton, half resolute and half exasperated, went to the head of the class and said, "Hi, I'm Mr. Payne, Dean of Students at The Grauer School. Is anyone willing to work with one of our students? We'd like to meet you." Back home on the coast, Clayton was "the man," but would he be cool out here? How cross-cultural is cool? Half-heartedly, two hands went up and two of our students attended at their desks. Clayton pressed on, "Anyone else? We drove 900 miles just to work with you. Who's willing?" Another hand popped up, and then another and another, as our students paired off with their Native American counterparts at their desks. It was reassuring to witness how powerful teachers could become, and how quickly trust could seep into the arena, when students are offered authentic choices. A few more hands went up until all but three or four students had partners. Then, the textbook was no longer a mere relic and no longer a foreign and cardboard article of oppression, but an object for sharing.

Some did not want to do the history lesson, and we didn't care. We had brought paper and colored pencils (along with a large duffle bag of basketballs and volleyballs), and encouraged anyone who wanted to draw. One student was intensely drawing, but looked reticent and angry. Colin. We studied his paper and noticed his native imagery of an eagle flying before the moon, free and powerful. We asked him about it and he reluctantly let us see more. The drawing got larger, and over the next 20 minutes filled the page. A sun emerged, exotic and beautiful. "You are an artist and you'll be important some day," somebody said. He sat up straighter. Then the drawing was done and something unexpected happened. He offered it to one of our students and then something even more unpredictable happened, he opened his book and began examining the actual assignment.

Around the room, our students were learning about their counterparts. "Do you know Navajo language," we asked one student. "Diné, not Navajo," she corrected. "Yes, from my grandmother." "What about your mother?" we wanted to know. "My mother explained other things to me. Like how love is bulshee." Many parents of this generation, not only here but on Indian reservations all over America, have turned to alcohol or drugs. And, as in many traditional societies, it is the grandparents who attempt to pass along the culture. The Navajo traditions are at least 700 years old and appear to be going extinct. The elders learned in the very hardest way that public school is a terrible place to entrust the passing along of these traditions. Would they be passed along at all?

"Maybe this language will be very valuable as less people know it," somebody suggested to her. "Like gold. There is not too much of it so it will be valuable." She smiled. There is a thawing in the room as we share.

In the next class, we create circles of desks for five or six students to gather around. Facing each other, they talk about their music, their families and the futures they may bear. It is as though some kind of balance is being restored.

Now the principal walks in carrying a yardstick in the way of a willow switch. He is an Anglo, the new superintendent spurned, exiling him out on the reservation rather than in a plum assignment back in Gallup. He raises his brow and we act preoccupied and a bit fumbling because we know what he is seeing does not meet with his expectations: the rows are all gone, the textbooks are closed, and the kids are animated and not "on task" at all.

His role is to keep order, so he calls over a Navajo student. It's the errant football player. "What are you doing?" he seethes, and the message is clear.

"Look how engaged they become in small councils, like around the Hogan," we say to the principal, pathetically. "It's great to try new teaching methods for connecting with the kids."

He nods. Who knows if he understands? He takes his

leave and, at the door, looks back at us and says, "It's all about politics."

Of course, he was right. And by the time the door set back on the doorjam eyes, blue and brown and green, were lighting up and we all had each other.

Next, like subversive activity, most of the class easily formed into mixed, intercultural pairs or triads, and we hardly had to ask most of the students to get their work done, because it was not about the textbook anymore. It was about taking selfies, sharing answers to the textbook questions, and swapping text message numbers and stories about parents and families. This is the way. It is about the connection. The invisible barrier is broken. The threat and despair in the room is almost gone and like magic, by the end of class, most of these students hand in their written assignments. Colin fist bumps Clayton on the way out, and just for a second they are looking at each other and sharing something. Suddenly, there is a way forward. Later, we asked a tribal official, "If you are serious about restoring native culture, why can't you get native teachers, and why do you have to rely upon citified principals and 23-year-old Teach for America teachers who leave every two years? Where are your own teachers?" We want to know: "Where are your people?"

Time after time in our work as teachers, we have witnessed the sheer delight students and teachers take in doing nothing more than circling around, eyes drawn together, and discovering one another. There is no greater miracle and it is a waste of time to look farther than that; nevertheless, since it can't be measured and monetized, people will keep trying. Textbook companies and academics and governments will keep trying. As James Conant phrased it a century ago, "No significant learning can occur without a significant relationship." It is the presence of significant relationships that makes learning matter.

So that was our day. But, we were returning the next day to a place where the teachers had been at the same school for an average of seven years, disappearing back to the Pacific coast as though we were just something the Indian students dreamed. The Navajo language doesn't even have a word for "ocean."

The Great Rift Valley, largest land form on earth.

"We have all a better guide in ourselves, if we would attend to it, than any other person can be."

—Jane Austen

Still We Wander

Have we accidently re-engineered our classroom methodologies to exclude students who don't learn like the teachers we hire? As we narrow the role and definition of classroom teacher, are we narrowing the definition of intelligence? What kinds of learning and knowing are we losing?

Every October is Attention Deficit and Hyperactivity Deficit (ADHD) Awareness Month. Also, it's the month for Halloween and autumn, with warm colors emerging everywhere. It's apple picking time too. I think I might have ADHD.

I guess I hope so. Quite a few people I know with ADHD are the extra-aware types. ADHD minds may want to learn or explore everything at once. They start out on a topic, then often associate almost anything to it. They are also incredibly open to discovery of every kind. And though it drives some teachers crazy, let's just be aware that wanting to return back home to the initial topic might be someone else's need, but not necessarily that of a person with ADHD.

October is a month of awareness. We start noticing things changing. It is autumn and the sunlight is decreasing and days are getting shorter. And the leaves make less and less sugar. Eventually, the chlorophyll pigments in leaves decrease and the green color in them begins to fade. In time, photosynthesis stops, and the veins at the bases of the leaf stems sometimes close, trapping sugars. As the chlorophyll fades, any yellow, orange, or gold pigments that are present in the leaves are revealed.

"This is a good time for wandering along the hillside," I suggest, and we abandon the lesson and pack up our writing journals. Perhaps we shall collect leaves to lay out into a collage, creating patterns. An ADHD mind may take broad, inexplicable, beautiful leaps and create amazing bridges. These kinds of minds may stare at clouds until they become like the Alps, at least mine did, and then ski away.

If someone were teaching us about ADHD the way most teachers are taught to teach, in accordance with California State Frameworks or in preparation for ERB or SAT tests, or the Chinese Gaokao exams, they might determine that the above observations are evidence of distraction or hyperactivity, perhaps even warranting medication. For some kids, it may be so, but the situation also is due in most part to our schools allowing precious little time and space for students to digress and discover, however naturally. This is a problem because so many teachers feel they are required to teach in straight lines, and to known outcomes, while many of our mind-wandering kids may never learn while seated still in rows, as if the words of the history teacher were filtered through an Ojibwa dream catcher. The world is filled with magnificent windows, and some students are captivated by them.

For those kids, teachers may prevent learning rather than allow it. And yet, most of us know at least one or two teachers who can somehow find spaces for students to make their own choices; teachers who mix up the methodologies and group formations, who are humble and Socratic, and who invite students to use their real voices and eyes. "Dreamcatcher" teachers.

ADHD-types and lateral thinkers are on topic, maybe just not the topic you require them to be on. They may not care to separate cognition from metacognition, art from science. Take heart though, in the right environment, even if that means outdoors, they will usually bring things back home to your topic if you really want them to, or if you insist. They might just prefer, while seated in classrooms for days on end, imagining themselves riding on the tip of a light beam while imagining themselves aboard a tram in Bern rumbling up the Kramgasse on their way to the patent office.

Ex-missionary in Tanzania Daudi Pederson re-discovered the Hadza tribe by lighting an oil drum filled with tobacco—the hunter gatherers came from miles around.

"Do you know the difference between education and experience? Education is when you read the fine print; experience is what you get when you don't."

—Pete Seeger

Pete Seeger
A Real Teacher

Is there such a thing as authentic teaching or authentic learning? How far can the teacher go to move instruction toward authentic accomplishments for students?

I didn't learn much in college. At least not in the first two years. I thought at the time that I had no real prospects to come from the education I was enduring and so might as well drop out. That summer though, I stumbled upon a book that changed everything. Not only in making me a better student, but ultimately in making me a better teacher. It was called *How to Play the 5-String Banjo*, written and self-published by Pete Seeger.

I didn't have a banjo. But in the back of the book were some references on how to make your own, so I ran around New York and New England gathering the parts. I then loosely followed Pete's instructions on banjo making and it felt like the first real thing I'd done in a while. I hardly knew how to play however, on the back of the book there was a quote from an 1800s banjo picker: "Can I read notes? Hell, there are no notes to a banjo, you just play it." So I did.

At college—with its learned professors and its straight A students—no matter what I wanted to study, there were always other kids who dwarfed my skills and knowledge. In the giant university halls of academia, learning seemed like an in-game and I admit I often downshifted, feeling low in confidence. What college appeared to be teaching me, and arguably at least one-third of all who start out in the university life, was that we probably wouldn't be particularly distinguished at anything they had to offer. I was living in a world of experts. But the way Pete presented it, learning was something for everyone and it had nothing to do with being compliant or getting a grade. To me, making things now seemed like it was for everyone. And making music was something for everyone.

Pete had been to England and France and found that music, analogous to what I had found about college, had become an in-game for the classicists who felt anything done by the common people was something "less." But for Pete, music-making was not just for concert halls and recording artists, it was for front porches and school assemblies. What Pete was saying in his self-published book was that you didn't need to be a formal, classically trained musician to get full access to music. Music comes from us, and is not reserved for the elite. We need only to allow it to come out, practice it, and then embrace it.

Luckily, as time went on, a number of other people also remembered that music was for front porches, campfires, and town squares, and that we could all have lovely partnerships even if we would not ever play at Lincoln Center or become stars. In fact, almost every sound you can make on any street corner in the country is close to folk music. If you get chased off the corner making that sound, it's even more folk music ... and I admit I've been chased off street corners with my students, as I'm sure Pete was many times.

We're all musicians if we're willing to be. With this approach, despite massive cuts to arts education, it would be impossible to keep music out of almost any classroom. For example, there can be music of spheres for math, national anthems for history, beta beats for physical education, and soft baroque for study sessions.

Here is a short list of Pete Seeger songs, either written, co-written, or introduced to national audiences by him:

We Shall Overcome
This Land is Your Land
Where have All the Flower's Gone
Turn, Turn, Turn
Tzena, Tzena, Tzena
Kisses, Sweeter than Wine
Wimoweh (Lion Sleeps Tonight)
Kumbaya
She'll be Coming 'Round the Mountain
Follow the Drinkin' Gourd
Sloop John B
The Midnight Special
On Top of Old Smokey

These fill in an indispensable mid-twentieth century American songbook for our students and younger teachers as well as create an indelible link between the social change and music of the twentieth century. At least as important is that these are songs that every one of our students can sing with their own voices. In addition, some of these songs such as "Wimoweh," "Follow the Drinkin Gourd," and "Turn Turn Turn," are deeply and hauntingly beautiful.

There aren't that many traditional folksingers in the country these days and I wonder if many of our students know what a folksinger's true role is. As a folksinger, Seeger was motivated by concerns for social justice, cross-cultural communication, and international peace, and so he performed a diversity of songs to any "folks" who'd listen. He lived to be very old. At some point, every American ought to know the life of this amazing individual who spread freedom and simple, necessary folk wisdom all over our country; the kind of wisdom that is now in our national DNA even for those who don't know where it came from.

I'd like to think a great school has some folk teachers willing to risk it all for some lessons that really reach students. A folk teacher would be one who was willing to step off the standards train now and then, to risk his/her very job just to hear the natural voices that students bring to class.

I read that in February 2009, the San Diego Unified School District officially extended an apology to Pete for trying to ban his earlier performances. Frankly, I don't know where we'd be without him. Most don't realize too that Pete was in World War II and fought for this country. Nevertheless, he was blacklisted from employment during the McCarthy era and almost starved playing for kids at schools and such, when he could hardly get work. One really cool thing to read is Pete's testimony before the U.S. Congress's House Un-American Activities Committee—McCarthy's bunch. They tried to get him to say he sang his songs for communists, and that he was un-American. His testimony, hysterically funny for its attitude, landed Pete in jail. Right here in America. Here is a bit of it:

> Pete: "I have sung in hobo jungles, and I have sung for the Rockefellers, and I am proud that I have never refused to sing for anybody."
>
> The McCarthy prosecutor, citing a newspaper ad: "Tonight—Bronx, hear Peter Seeger and his guitar, at Allerton Section housewarming." He continues, "May I ask you whether or not the Allerton Section was a section of the Communist Party?"
>
> Pete: "Sir, I refuse to answer that question, whether it was a quote from *The New York Times* or the *Vegetarian Journal*."
>
> The McCarthy prosecutor: "My question was whether or not you sang at these functions of the

Communist Party. You have answered it inferentially, and if I understand your answer, you are saying you did."

Pete, in a classic sting: "I know many beautiful songs from your home county, Carbon, and Monroe, and I hitchhiked through there and stayed in the homes of miners."

This strategy was considered to be contempt of Congress. And as a result, for almost 20 years no major TV network would allow Pete on the air.

On YouTube you can see him strumming a handmade, fretless banjo, and singing, "What Did You Learn in School Today." This video can give you a sense of how provocative he could be. Of course, when someone has enough insight, like Pete did, many others will almost always find him to be provocative.

As America developed mass food, mass culture and mass education, and problems got bigger, Pete kept things on a human scale, valuing the kind of learning you can only get when you use your hands. One good development in education is called "The Maker Movement." This approach brings back the original do-it-yourself culture to our nation, and is re-engaging people across the country in making things like metalwork, woodwork, and traditional arts and crafts. This is also reflected by sustainable, organic gardens that are popping up on campuses across the country, as well as by natural habitats like local riverbeds and corridors so many schools are adopting.

As if anticipating all this, in 1969, Pete and others purchased a large, 106-foot sloop and spent literally years traveling up and down the Hudson River, with his banjo, until people understood the need to keep toxins out of the waterway. He taught virtually every person in the nation who was sane that rivers should not catch on fire and he is credited with the passage of one of the most landmark bills in U.S. history: The Clean Water Act.

Into his 90s, Pete protested every week outside his Hudson River house in Beacon, New York, and people would pass by and say, "Alright Pete!" This great American folk legend died on January 27, 2014 at 94. They said he was out chopping wood just a few days before. Maybe if chopping wood were required curriculum for middle school kids, they'd be a whole lot more ready when they got to high school.

He was the old soul among us. Do you recognize him?

Something hidden. Go and find it. Go and look
Behind the ranges—
Something lost behind the Ranges. Lost and waiting
For you. Go.

—Rudyard Kipling

The Wounded Ones
(A Winter Night With No Lights)
ERIC NELSON 1981 – 2013

Working with teens, how do we treat the dark ones? To what extent do conformity and "standard" expectations force our students to lose their way?

As an elementary school student, his teachers complained he couldn't sit still. That didn't change much even as he got older. I knew him when he was a student at The Grauer School. People just wanted to be around him. He was the old soul among us, always understanding, quiet and calm. Observing much, hovering in the midst, patient with a knowing smile. He wore mostly black clothing. Frequently that included a black leather vest. Maybe, too, black nail polish, a black bandana and a shark tooth necklace. Do you recognize him?

Was Eric so bad he was good, or so good he was bad? Once we were skiing through a snowstorm in Yosemite and he was the one to keep everyone's attitudes upbeat, the positive voice, always cool. But what of a person whose end goal is not to achieve but merely to explore?

Eric Nelson stood for so many of our teens, an identity searching for a place. He and youths like him challenge us as teachers as we attempt to honor them in their efforts to find patterns in their meanderings. What greater challenge could there be for a teacher?

Before his attendance at The Grauer School, Eric had never wanted to go to a school. But on the day of his graduation, in 1999, he and his class prepared a large banner which sprawled across the faculty room wall reading: "Thank you, Teachers. We will appreciate you some day." Like so many high school kids, Eric was an innocent visitor to a world where few people really need teens, so he tread lightly, digging around the roots. For teens like this, the best a high school can be is a compassionate gathering place, a place for connecting and growing up—not a place of judgment or false competition.

The conventional path for teen life must have appeared narrow and uninspired for Eric. Still, there had to be some uplifting pursuits, if only he could find them. Eric was a seeker. He was a gentle, good guy. His former teacher, Sawako Nakayasu, said, "The last time I saw him he took me to an abandoned reservoir somewhere not far from school where we walked atop the precarious ruins of the old structure."

When he was a senior in high school, eventually he found art and we were talking about college in Minnesota. That story, right up to the end, is told poignantly by his mother, Annette:

> *His photography often found beauty in things the rest of us would fail to see until his photo caught it. He has sold some of his photos and exhibited. A neighbor had recently given him a new camera stating that he had a heart of gold and that they knew that he would appreciate the camera. Eric cried.*

She continued emotionally,

> *He was absolutely enamored with a vacant mill in Minneapolis that he discovered about a year ago. I just*

couldn't 'see' the beauty in this particular building but it kept drawing him back. No one knew that he had headed there the day before he died. His final photo was taken at about 4:30PM. I imagine that he was leaving—not even Eric would be there on a winter night with no lights anywhere in the area. He fell 30 feet when a part of the structure gave out, badly broke his femur and laid in the snow in below freezing temperatures for hours, alone. I had to go back and see this building in the day—I hoped it would erase the horrific images imprinted in my memory. We found his cell phone in the snow about a foot away from where he was laying. The night before he died, we expected to see him by about 8:30 PM. When he didn't show up, call, or answer his phone, something told me that he was at the mill. Jim and I arrived in the freezing cold to a totally dark, ominous, run down, looming structure. We tried to find our way around. At one point, we backed our car out of an area in the back of the building because we were afraid we'd get stuck after we bumped into something metal under the snow on the ground. [A camera?] At that time, we had no idea that Eric was laying on the ground about 10 feet from us. We called 911 to see again if they would come look. Minneapolis already had police en route since Eric's phone pinged in the area. They instructed us to stay where we were and two officers headed on foot closer to the building with flashlights. Soon I saw emergency lights behind us—I knew they had found him. We were not allowed to get close to the scene. I imagine that they were trying to spare us from seeing a sight that we would never be able to erase. Eric's heart was still beating but stopped when they put him in the ambulance. As always, he fought to hang on. We sat in trauma with him for several hours as they tried desperately to raise his body temperature and get his heart to maintain beating on its own. Fifteen people surrounded him trying to save him. No one can fathom the death of their child but the thought of him laying badly hurt and alone in the dark and bitter cold is something that haunts me and repeatedly breaks my heart. Eric did not deserve such a tragic heartbreaking end—he knew enough heartbreak in his young life. I am happy that he had recently hit a place of belonging. Work was going well. He had new friends who seemed to appreciate him. His attitude was upbeat, hopeful, encouraged, positive. He was considerate, funny, responsible. He was looking forward to the future. He was so excited about an upcoming family trip to Denver and had planned photographing around Red Rocks.

Here is the truth: seekers suffer. Where do you head in this world of school and work if you have not found your true north? It is astonishing how quickly our schools and society will turn on a teen who will not abide by the narrow rules and confines of acceptable adolescence—such a bizarre concept as it is. What if life calls you, truly draws you down a path with no rhyme or reason, or to some netherworld, or fairytale or trespass, and you are on this path and can never know if it is even the right path but you keep going and keep hoping, pressing on, never knowing where it might take you? What if we find ourselves drawn to insights and sensitivities with no utility? An unworkable, old mill?

"A thing you never have to teach a child is metaphor," explains Jay Griffiths. So why must we keep re-teaching it to adults? Griffiths continues, "Metaphor is a stance of the mind where children seem to dwell happily. But ours is an age where only what is measured, costed, counted, and accounted is considered valuable."

Who can say what ancient voice called Eric from the urban

ruins of Minneapolis? Was it the vacant silo, the dry smell, the tangles of machinery, pipes and gears? Was this the childhood fantasia, the heroic quest he and so many others miss growing up? What would I, his teacher, say to Eric if we had met there one day?

We will never fully know Eric's attraction to the mill; the rusty, decaying shadow of a world gone. But as his old teacher, there is some peace in understanding that he heard a calling, followed it, and found home.

Author's daughter Audrey, China, 2008

"Neither by suppression of the material streaming out of the consciousness nor by permanent surrender to the unshaped infinity of the unconscious, but rather through affectionate attention to these hidden sources—thus have all the great artists worked."

—Herman Hesse

Zenbells
(The Art of Paying Attention)

Is "Alright, quiet down over there," achieving what we want—and what presumptions does this command reveal in educators? Are educators and parents using much of what we know about consciousness and concentration? What is essential to great teaching: providing great information or creating a great environment for learning?

Over the course of earning three academic degrees, I sat through dozens of courses on education. None of them paid much attention to the practice of paying attention to students. Attention seemed to always be presumed, as though we're all masterfully present with one another. And that attention was to be managed rather than practiced, controlled rather than understood, presumed or demanded rather than engaged in. Why then, do some of the most ancient and revered teaching techniques involve nothing more than teaching students and disciples the deceptively refined art of paying attention? Why are these age-old arts rarely practiced in our classrooms? Is "Alright, quiet down over there," really achieving what we want?

Bells figure prominently in schooling. Bell systems throughout the world send out cracks in the middle of millions of conversations, thoughts in development, paragraphs, and reflective moments. At our school, our program called (with some amusement) Zenbells, plays very soft baroque or natural environmental sound when a period ends. As a consequence, we don't see doors bolting open with kids escaping classes— thoughts get resolved, or they can, and students and teachers move with some intentionality and presence.

A few years ago, I noticed a Tibetan singing bowl in Vancouver's Chinatown. Although singing bowls and other meditative sound making have some pockets of popularity around the world, they are mostly disregarded by teachers and in schools of education. However, the singing bowl has been widely used for personal and group contemplative practices. For something like 3,000 years these sounds have been effective in producing audibles of a therapeutic, calming and even healing nature. And so, I purchased the bowl.

One day I brought this bowl into our weekly school assembly, sat down on the fireplace hearth, and held it out before our 200 seated students, teachers and guests. Then, moving the wooden handle around and around the rim of the brass bowl, a simple sound began to rise. Gradually, a second and then a third harmonic overtone built up upon the initial, simple tone. It was captivating. Concealing my insecurity with this action, I let the bowl gain in clarity as the sound grew steadier. Apparently the students arrived at the same curiosity as the room quieted. Since then, I've been practicing this technique every week.

I love watching the talky, diverse group of students come into a sense of unity, such as this bowl invites, if not induces. I love watching the students and teachers in the assembly room as chaos transforms into a pure focus, each time a little differently. As I watch, it becomes clear that we do not even need content to engage in pure teaching experiences, but that real teaching consists essentially of the study of students and their states of mind.

As Rick Hanson says in his beautiful book *Buddha's Brain: The Practical Neuroscience of Happiness, Love and Wisdom*, "attention shapes the brain." And it is the real teacher who can deeply attend.

There are stages of attention-getting when we use the singing bowl. At first, people become increasingly aware of the spreading of silence across the room, and they tend to look around to confirm it. I normally continue to keep the bowl singing for a few seconds after that, even after the first silence has been achieved, and we develop a collective, shared focus on the immaculate tone. Then, as I stop playing the bowl, it continues ringing for a while as the sound dissipates into nothingness. Pure silence. I enjoy allowing a few seconds of just this, making an effort to trust my patience even if my practice seems foolish or pointless to some. Any teacher unwilling to make a fool of himself will not get far. Over the years, my confidence in the presence and attunement of the group as it attempts to be silent has grown increasingly unforced, patient, and genuine. This is the type of silence you can hear when you quiet your mind, when you quiet the space on both sides of your ears! It is the only time all week our entire campus is silent.

I understand that some people eschew this kind of practice and quiet. Likewise, sometimes the temptation to end the silence too soon is high or I become unconfident about the level of attention we have attained. Even so, I try to study the faces carefully. I try to study the silence and listen into it.

As teachers, we routinely demand of our students, "Pay attention," as though the path to attentiveness is obvious, understood, and easy. It is none of these. Real attention means there are quiet voices but also quiet minds. As a teacher, I try not to confuse a quiet room with necessarily clear and receptive minds. But I know many times in the past I have failed to make this distinction as there is no getting away from the terrible

The number of Chinese seeking entry into U.S.
independent K-12 schools is swelling.

"Yes, yellow birds know where they should perch. How can a person not be of the same wisdom as a bird."

—Confucius

The Gaokao Cowboy

How can we make every class like a lab where genuine discovery is possible? Is our role as teachers and parents to help kids fit in or stand out? And should America be more like China?

Around the turn of the millennium, at our school, we said if our students don't know about China, they won't know about the world, and so we planned our first trip there. We were going to the land of Confucius! Lao Tzu! Back then, you could still find there apothecaries carrying rare birds' blood, dried lizard organs and endangered antelope remedies smuggled across the Mongolian border. And when we walked out of our hotel that first morning someone tried to sell us a leopard skin. Beijing was still the home of silk merchants, pearl growers, jade carvers. No more.

We were the very first Americans to set foot in the Shanghai University Middle School. (In China a middle school is what we call a secondary school.) China was opening up then right before our eyes, though we could still grasp ancient images carried through the ages on perfumed winds, rice houses and exotic merchants all about Shanghai's old town. I bought a ball cap for a dollar. Less than a decade later, it was an altogether new ballgame, especially in schooling.

In 2013, I returned as a part of a group of independent American educators hand selected by a Chinese educational foundation for our potential partnership with prominent Chinese high schools. We headed for Nanjing. Nanjing is a city known for top Chinese education. Nanjing's famous Purple Mountain, once considered idyllic countryside, is now surrounded by some 30 universities.

Chinese education was becoming dynamic for one of the first times in its history, exploring new pathways. There is little tradition of independent education, but a budding interest laden with potential for cognitive dissonance. Upon arrival, as dignitaries, we were received around a giant conference table by the provincial minister of education. "Would you ever be interested in introducing a small schools concept in China," I asked the minister, "for instance, schools of around 200 students each, or a school within a school?"

"Yes," came back through our translator, Jeff. "He is interested in this idea."

"That means 'No', right?" I said to Jeff.

"No, he means, Yes." I wondered if Jeff really meant, "Yes, he means No." By that time, after a week on the road meeting officials, I had determined that "Yes" means either "Yes," "Perhaps," or "No," and that "No" was not used.

"Got it," I signaled Jeff. As such, we were oriented as well as could be for bureaucracy the scale of which we could only pretend to grasp. But Elvis was already in the arena: Across China, across Asia, Western-style schools and colleges had been popping up. In Hong Kong, South Korea, Vietnam and China, British and American schools were teaming with local counterparts and forming independent schools.

In fact, all across China, Western-style schools and colleges were popping up. Enlightened Chinese educators were seeking escape from rote learning and high stakes testing. For instance, the centuries-old Harrow School of England established a branch in Hong Kong. One of its Hong Kong school parents echoed the exact sentiment I had read about: "Harrow takes a much more holistic view than many other schools in Hong Kong, not just focusing on academic results but also putting a great deal of emphasis on developing each individual into a citizen of the world" (Ang & Kwok, 2012). The Waldorf School in Chengdu, a reaction to the rigidity of Chinese schooling, has a five-year waiting list. Of course, there are things about Western-style teaching that might not be perfect in every culture. "American notions about teacher status and prestige, like fast food and reality TV, seem to have been exported worldwide, infecting the field on a global scale," noted Professor Rosetta Marantz Cohen of Smith College.

The next day was the centerpiece of our week. We were to visit Nanjing No. 1, a secondary school with 10,000 students, on the occasion of their 103rd anniversary. We were ushered in through the venerable, old gateway lined with bowing students in blue blazers, past the fountain with floating lotus flowers, past the classic pagoda, and were seated in the grand courtyard arena where the culture was about to get real. Presently, a procession ascended to the giant Nanjing #1 School stage, "Blazing Saddles" blaring on the PA. Curvy cheer squad coeds in red cowboy hats and white bobby sox danced in unison, then the school hip hop boyz popped and locked to American-style rap music sung in Chinese. It was the new China, the winning of the West. After some speeches and a triumphant giant screen film featuring Mao in a train, we crossed the quad past the school's old, empty pagoda, and entered the four-story school. We filed into a ninth grade class studying Advanced Placement (A.P.) chemistry in English. A local newspaper reporter approached me: "I don't understand why all the Chinese here want to take American A.P. classes," she prompted. "What is so good about them?"

In China, schools traditionally have not empowered students to be active participants in learning. I replied, "An Advanced Placement course has a lot of content. You can't really study much in depth. You must keep charging forward all semester long to cover all the required topics."

We settle down for the chemistry lesson. The teacher had set up a demo at the front of the room. Since the students had no supplies, she called it a "Mini-lab." Two students helped the teacher demonstrate how the making of sodium compounds can produce fire. This experiment is an old standby. The only trouble was, the first three times she attempted to make fire, it failed to ignite. Rather than asking, "Why has the fire failed to ignite?" and then treat the situation as though something might be worthy of actual investigation, she just pressed on. At last, on the fourth try, a beautiful, chemical combustion jumped into life. It was a multiple choice, fill-in lab. There are a number of background assumptions in this whole exercise, such as: discovery and science are predictable and follow a linear path, knowledge acquisition occurs along a set start and finish time, the role of students is to passively observe what everyone already knows, and the role of the teacher is to impart information devoid of both emotion and significant relationships. Naturally, they are background assumptions because they are rarely acknowledged here in China and, in fact, in many national schooling systems.

After class, the reporter approached me once again, "What is so good with this A.P.?"

"A.P. courses," I risked, "can stifle deep investigation of any topic and replace the processes of discovery and personal investigation with pursuit of a test score. Nine months in the classroom and, at the end, you and the teacher are judged by a single test result." And I wonder, *What is so Western about this test?*

Written examinations as determinants of educational attainment may add efficiency and reliability in sorting our students, but they also may have rather enormous negative side effects. In the United States, A.P. students get caught in a cycle of sleep depravation and overwork. Yet, high school ranking services still equate the percentage of students taking A.P. courses with a school's quality.

Pronounced "gow-cow," the revered and feared Gaokao — properly called the Chinese National Higher Education Entrance Examination — is the world's most grueling national high school test. The exam takes three days and determines nothing less than whether and where you go to college and what your major will be. Whole city blocks are closed off to maintain quiet testing conditions. Airplanes have been rerouted. There are only enough college seats for between 60 to 75 percent of applicants, although this number appears to be increasing. The stakes are high.

So it may come as no surprise that the number of Chinese seeking entry into U.S. independent K-12 schools is swelling. Chinese international students more than doubled between 2007 and 2012, according to statistics from the Institute of International Education. And over the previous five years, most of the U.S. growth in international enrollments has come from China as parents there try to give their children the best opportunity to gain higher education. In addition to the educational benefits for their children, there are financial benefits. For example, it costs a Chinese family twice as much to send their child to an independent school in China than to an American independent school.

Alternatively, Chinese state schools find that they can collaborate with U.S. independent schools, dedicating a wing in their own building in which all courses are taught in English. In this way, they can steer their graduates towards U.S. educational institutions. So rewards to American cooperating independent schools are considerable.

There is a saying that when you're one in a million in China, there are 1,300 others identical to you. Uniformity and predictability tend to be acculturated priorities with numbers like this. Perhaps otherwise there would be chaos in many social situations. Chinese high schools can have up to 10,000 students and class sizes can range from 35 to 50, so expressions of individuality can be disruptive. There is little room for dissent.

In America, independent education is the oldest continuing form of schooling, not public education. Independent schooling has been ongoing since well before the American Revolution and still today serves one out of every eleven students nationwide. In addition to independent education, there are various other alternatives to public education. One in nine students nationwide gets schooling through alternative ways such as home schools, religious schools, and charter schools.

Today in China, there are a few independent schools for students needing special services, but little else. China has virtually no viable concept for small schools, a reality that helps keep in place a reliance on standardized exams.

Traditional Chinese education featured "sishu," small private schools serving local needs. Confucius himself taught in this kind of schoolhouse. For many families, a sishu education was a form of stature and prestige. For some, the sishu offered preparation for the famed civil service exams, precursors to the Gaokao. But by the 1950s, this form of private education had been discontinued in China instead of being reformed and improved upon. However, the standardized examination emphasis remained.

Change is still underway in Chinese education as they investigate Western concepts like school culture and trending educational technologies. Today, Chinese teachers are often found with laptops. So far, they are used primarily to make the teachers, not the students, more efficient, although there is often a student computer lab on campuses. Yet, even less well-off students normally have a computer at home in order to have a real chance at college.

After the chemistry lesson, outside in the hallway, our group found the school principal and the Communist Party leader, smiling. "Surely the A.P. is more liberating than the Gaokao," I am explaining to the reporter as we take our places. "The Gaokao judges students' entire schooling on one exam. At least with A.P., you get to have exams on various subjects (i.e. math, English, science). But it is hardly representative of a whole education. It's just more standardization, more centralized control, and more high stakes exams—a growing trend across the U.S. People often treat the College Board (purveyor of the A.P.) as a government agency." I try to explain, "What's American about the College Board is far more political than educational. It is an extremely well funded special interest group exerting enormous influence on the national funding priorities."

We all moved down the hallway into the large conference room and, once we were seated, the principal welcomed us and the forum was underway. Around the long, gleaming conference table, such as I found in each of the seven schools I had visited around China, we were seated across from Nanjing teachers and parents. And there, projected large and vibrant on the screen at the front of the room were the words: "Forum on A.P." I got a lump in my throat. The big announcement was that we are gathering to celebrate the adoption of the program I have just bashed in the press. I think: *Is this okay? Should I be speaking to the press in China?* I had no idea. This is a communist country. *Don't they throw people in jail for dissidence like this?*

Now the principal is detailing with great pride how A.P. studies represent the school's aspirations towards the creation of a new culture of innovation and freedom. As an educator, my question is this: Since when has the taking of A.P. exams even remotely equated to the development of educational innovation? Really, they do just the opposite. A.P. curricula incubate compliance and standardization far more than creative expression, human understanding, or liberty. It's Gaokao lite! A.P. credits are also being dropped by some colleges, and often cited as central causes of student burnout. Yet, A.P. classes produce measurable results since they are fundamentally test based—you either pass the exam and get the college units, or not. But measurability is not the same as social worth or value.

Now a parent at the table is saying how American universities are the best in the world. How "American educators have more liberties." We know they want their kids in our American schools. We also know that a school in China cannot easily get accredited by any American accreditation agency. Hence, the Chinese school students do not have easy access to our universities. In this sense, A.P. tests provide pre-approved units at many U.S. universities. The Chinese have found a loophole into U.S. colleges. What's more, this could mean billions for the College Board.

Questions are going around the table, courtesies exchanged, and yet I feel trapped in this room. Should I even offer my ideas? Will the Chinese, in their current period of prosperity, quickly scoop the best of whatever they find in all of our schools? Would they bring American educational technology and methods home until they mastered them independently, and then drop us like a colony depleted of its gold. Were they already doing this? American Universities were going up all over China. I fully understood this question could cause me to be reviled in both nations, but I was wondering: Were we pawns or dignitaries?

After the A.P. forum, Mr. Lee, the Nanjing principal invited us out to dinner. Sitting there, as we all raised our glasses of "maotai" in a toast, I finally understood that what breaks my heart is not that the U.S. and China are both pouring such precious resources into turning schools into state monoliths that will surely be wasteful, bureaucratized, and impersonal.

What breaks my heart is how lost I know so many teens to be. How much pain and loneliness they can feel during these years. How much promise and how fine the sensitivity is at this age. How much better they would do if there were giving, listening, warm-hearted schools rather than gigantic, systematized models of standardization.

"Tonight I have a special announcement," Principal Lee says. "Today the newspaper came to our school to cover our model A.P. program. The A.P. program is one of the keys to our future. It is the best of the East and the West. It can help take our school to an internationally prominent level." He raises his glass again. "When the newspaper story is printed tomorrow, the whole province will know of our accomplishment."

"Gan bei," we all toast. "Gone by," it sounds like. "Gone by," and I drink it down.

A bakery in Mexico has lessons in math, art, chemistry, and history.

Photo by Sophie Oller, The Grauer School

"It is easy to forget that a deep connection to nature provides the inspiration for genuine democratic thinking."

—Peter Senge

Too Nice a Day to Stay Inside

What could be the best roles and purposes for free time in the classroom and the school day? What if we could restore play as a fundamental way of learning in the classroom?

B ack in 1999, after eight years of expanding our shop front we finally moved The Grauer School onto our dream site: five, green, coastal acres in Encinitas. It was then that we made an unexpected finding about typical California suburban kids: many did not know how to have outdoor fun or use unstructured time. We thought we'd see them running, chasing, throwing, falling. But instead, they stood around, looked into their computer screens, hung in corners of the field and slouched on couches in the school lobby.

This problem had never occurred to any of us. Since I grew up running pretty much all day long, and since my parents' primary form of discipline consisted of the mantra: "Get outside!" I had assumed there was something instinctual about play and that, if you left kids alone, they would just do it. However, in the case of many, the play had been drummed out of them through tightly managed schedules, too much homework, too many digital devices, too many curricular standards and benchmarks, too little time in nature, too little sleep, and too much parenting and schooling. "I'm opening the door to prison and you're running back in!" I nagged the kids.

> ... A year passed. I went out for a walk during morning classes on a winter Monday. It was mid-period, a clear balmy San Diego day. A door opened up and two boys went running out, then more students meandered, some together, some alone. One of the teachers was letting his students out for an unscheduled break and they took to the outdoors like water on a sponge ...

Early in my career, I used to think, "Keep them busy" and "We only have a few periods a day" and "Those parents expect their kids to get instruction every minute." But now, decades later, after thousands of hours spent with teens and their teachers, I don't think that way any more. Besides, brain research shows that a break of about four minutes every 20 minutes or so tends to allow for maximum mental efficiency. "Neuroscientists, developmental biologists, psychologists, social scientists, and researchers from every point of the scientific compass now know that play is a profound biological process," said Stuart Brown of Stanford, whose home office happens to be a treehouse. But must it really take neuroscientists to understand the obvious, explained around the year 400 B.C. by Plato: "Do not then train youths by force and harshness, but direct them to it by what amuses their minds so that you may be better able to discover with accuracy the peculiar bent of the genius of each." I wish I'd understood all that my first year teaching middle school back in the 70s, back when I obsessed on my curriculum but not on my students' learning needs.

> ... On one side of the field seven boys were weaving in and out of each other, further apart, then back again, several of them moving up the bank of a hill, roving like a pack. I had spent time observing wild horses up in South Dakota, and these boys' movements reminded me of those majestic animals. On the other side of the

field, five girls gradually moved under the shade of the holly oak tree forming a close circle of conversation and connection. Everyone seemed to be moving as nature intended. It was a veritable field day for gender studies. Then a boy wandered over to the group of girls, and from a distance it looked like they could have been talking in sign language since they used so many hand gestures...

Nothing teaches youths to self-organize and learn to socialize like play in true open space. All but the best teachers I ever see are unable to teach to open space, if not fearful of it. Children learn to discern roughhousing from real fighting by eye contact, expressions, and the kinds of sounds they make. Try that online! Boys are generally much more aware of the importance of rough and tumble play in establishing dominance while girls are much more likely to see it as simple play, and they avoid shows of supremacy.

Jean Piaget noted, "Play is the answer to how anything new comes about." Kids are essentially good at learning games through free play, which is the most natural thing in the world for them, though this has been removed or sanitized from so many environments. It seems unclear why so many teachers, parents, and curriculum writers think students learn best when they are kept in chairs all day long, or that they won't learn necessary things if they are not being taught or umpired or restricted. "Children's play is not sports and should be deemed their most serious activity," noted Montaigne as far back as the French Renaissance. (Montaigne was awakened in his castle daily by musicians.) When we over-regulate students we prevent the formation of group dynamics, prevent the formation of a sense of social ecology, prevent necessary social learning, and obscure the students' intrinsic inclination to seek learning. In 2014, Alison Gopnik at UC Berkeley showed how students who are given no instructions at all are more likely to come up with novel solutions to problems. Sugata Mitra showed no less in the world famous "Hole in the Wall Experiment." But we don't need scholarly research to tell us what, happily, the teacher of those students on break that day seemed to grasp intuitively: Kids need open space.

> . . . After a while, the students moved back in to the classroom and I didn't know exactly why. There was no bell. Their time out on the green was no longer than 5-7 minutes out of a 100-minute period, but the students were calmer and actually happy to go back to some direct instructional time. To the casual observer, it appeared they did this because they wanted to, the most natural behavior in the world . . .

Kids need movement. Teenagers who spend time in the gym will see a benefit in the classroom. Researchers from all over the world keep showing how rigorous movement and exercise increases performance on standardized tests in English, math and science. Even mild exercise improves the brain health and the ability to think.

Alternatively, the lack of physical movement has an impact on the brain. For instance, as reported in The New York Times, scientists at Wayne State University School of Medicine showed that many of the neurons in the brains of sedentary rats sprouted far more new tentacle-like arms known as branches. In active rats, branches connect healthy neurons into the nervous system. But these sedentary rat neurons sprouted more branches than normal neurons would have, making them more sensitive to stimuli and apt to zap scattershot messages into the nervous system. In effect, these neurons had changed in ways that made them likely to overstimulate the sympathetic nervous system. That sounds just like ADHD.

But do we really need brain science and big data to tell us what is before our eyes? One of my favorite teaching stories comes from the great philosopher, William James. At the start of the philosophy spring semester final exam at Harvard, a student, Gertrude Stein, wrote at the top of her exam book:

> *Dear Professor James,*
> *I am so sorry but really I do not feel a bit like an examination paper in philosophy to-day.*

And she left.

It was too nice a day to stay inside and write a final exam. James gave her the highest grade in his class. No matter that her action may have illustrated James' teaching on the "temporal sequence of undetermined alternative possibilities." James evidently understood that there was a much more important lesson in philosophy and education to teach that day: freedom is a basic human need. Why do we fear it?

The circle is the original classroom. Students gather at eye level in California coastal sage and maritime chaparral.

"There's a thread you follow. It goes among
things that change. But it doesn't change.
People wonder about what you are pursuing.
You have to explain about the thread.
But it is hard for others to see.
While you hold it you can't get lost.

Tragedies happen; people get hurt
or die; and you suffer and get old.
Nothing you do can stop time's unfolding.
You don't ever let go of the thread."

—William Stafford (*The Way It Is*)

Tree Stumps

What new kinds of classroom organizations might we try? Would teaching in natural spaces result in a different kind of human development? What can we do with these possibilities?

We preserved two acres of native habitat behind our school.

Our original school site had been in a shopping mall. The sort of place where, when you looked at it, nothing seemed capable of any origin. So for some years, I wanted to create a gathering space back there behind the school site. A council of sorts. Spaces like that are age-old, and they tend to develop in camps, tribal areas, war zones, and the wilderness. But I didn't want to disrupt the natural space back there. Instead, I wanted the council space to fit into the ecosystem.

It was one of those things that you mull over for some years, lightly, because you want the solution to come out naturally and unforced. You trust the idea will unfold if you let it. At last, one morning, the idea was ready. "We need to call around and get some tree stumps," I said to Tracy in the office. "We have to create a gathering circle in the habitat corridor." One fault of mine is that I sometimes demand when I think I'm asking. I'm working on humility, but it's a process.

"Where do you come up with this stuff?" she replied.

"I just know," I said.

She rolled her eyes. One thing we've been successful at in our school is taking the relationships we might expect to exist in a family or tribe and employ them right in the workplace. According to Edgar Schein, one of the nation's top organizational development experts, that's a great thing. Of course, whether this is optimal or whether it even matters, hardly any school even imagines functioning as a family or tribe.

I understood a tribal area was not normal. Instead, as school leaders, we are implored in virtually every professional publication nationwide to "switch the school's workflow to a digital platform," while we use "the six steps of consensus building," and to cover the "nine benchmarks standards" for teaching art. And the only conceivable reason for this is that curriculum writers have given up on the idea there can be authentic face time or empathic communication in a classroom. That the large, impersonal design of today's comprehensive schools is embedded in our collective, national consciousness is hardly even questioned.

(For the record, I also understood that the appropriate government agencies could object to the circle, or that it could be an attractive nuisance, or have legal issues. All of that.)

The circle, or council, has been the foundation of many cultures, and may well be the genesis of the concept of school. Now I had finally realized that what I'd wanted all along was a circle of tree stumps to sit on. My colleague, Simon, and I stomped around back behind the school and agreed upon a natural clearing that was big enough for a council. Then we called up our neighbor, Kent, who said he had three or four stumps he could drop off. That was a start.

Schools having neighbors who drop by could strike many as anachronistic, if not dangerous. Likewise, the notion of a council among students in the woods might also seem anachronistic, if not sententious, if not dangerous. The headlines about schools at the time were primarily on technology, immigration, or nationwide curriculum—big global movements with big money behind them. But I was holding on to the notion that education could primarily be a relationship between a teacher and a student. Whatever it was that made anyone think that educational technology or centralized authorities could improve upon a few students seated in a circle in a natural environment, I don't know. In council, eye to eye, there is time for silence, and time for ideas to percolate out of that. We could notice our straight-line expressions as they opened up into a circle, three-D. Someone could express their embarrassment about a new haircut, or edgy secrets could come out, or they could say how stupid the assignment was, and then we could attend to the real work. Of course, Montessori students have been doing this for around a century, as well as Phillips Exeter students around the Harkness table. There are pockets of it all over the world and, the more you look into it the more you will find that most people wish they were in one of them. This is not likely to be the subject of a major, longitudinal research experiment, though, nor will it attract grant dollars.

But there is some scientific research basis for it. For instance, here is something we know about learning: if students have their minds in an alpha state they are ready to engage mentally, recall things well, be creative, and be empathic.

Here are some things that can help produce an alpha state in the brain:

- A high trust, low threat environment
- Guided imagery and long, slow breathing
- Wind blowing through pine trees

Here are some things that tend not to:
- Criticism, ego, and judgment
- High stakes, standardized exams
- "Noise," like heavy metal music, crowds, or traffic

"The only real valuable thing is intuition," Einstein said. "The most beautiful thing we can experience is the mysterious. It is the source of all true art and all science. He to whom this emotion is a stranger, who can no longer pause to wonder and stand rapt in awe, is as good as dead: his eyes are closed."

Almost none of this "Einsteinian" experience is consciously made to be a part of a normal school classroom environment. But it could be. The pursuit of intuition is life changing, as it invites new discoveries, deeper forms of knowing, and perhaps finding a deeper purpose. When we are in these frames of mind—alpha state, open, intuitive—we start to notice forgotten forms of learning like paradox, serendipity, and the connection between the heart and mind. Coincidences seem to be happening to us again. Answers become open questions.

When I am ruler of world education, declaring answers to be questions will be my sole ambition. For many students who naturally seek this alpha state, just plain hanging out is easiest and most accessible on platforms like Instagram or World of Warcraft, but in those places they may never look into the eyes of another human. So, a circle of stumps . . .

The next day, as I helped our neighbor Kent unload the stumps, I thought, if I were to suggest to the U.S. Secretary of Education that schools needed to give students time sitting in nature on tree stumps and developing intuitive thought, he would of course think I was mad. Especially since *curriculum compacting* had become the millennial buzzword—we weren't hearing about curriculum expanding or even intelligence expanding—the game was to figure out how to rip through the curricular requirements.

Everywhere I travelled, in all corners of the world, whether affluent or disadvantaged, I was finding teachers largely focused on their ever-increasing workload and ever-decreasing time as they attempted in good faith to comply with a rigid lineup of state and national requirements. We are making ourselves exhausted.

That year, that past June, there had been some great buzz about The Green School in Bali, where lessons were held in open-sided bamboo pods. The general concept at The Green School was to focus on the whole child and to be a place for students to develop intrinsic purposes. Kids and teachers went on silent retreats together. But it was not likely that state and district school superintendents would be on any of those retreats. Green School had re-awakened to the idea that teaching can be a deepening relationship between students and teachers. Good thing it was in Bali, a place where people were willing to imagine it. I wondered, had the most obvious forms of education and intelligence development become the most obsolete and unworkable, ridiculous even?

Psychiatrists and brain researchers show how, in an absence of stress, creative, open-ended explorations can be the source of enormous adolescent innovation, passion, and social engagement. Perhaps we do need psychiatrists to remind us of our dreams, the dreams every one of us have had ... to tell us that forest pathways and tree branches and tracks enchant anyone who is young ...or who somehow stays young? That the young are drawn to mazes and to anything that winds or spirals or springs . . . and to nonsense, which is of course essential to sense . . . That they are compelled by anything that is a quest or a hunt, and they believe in magic only inasmuch as it is real, until teachers and fearful parents rear it out of them . . .

Much of the decision-making we do as adults is made in the unconscious mind, and those decisions are already made before we realize we have made them. Understandings, judgments, and beliefs that we often can not empirically verify or rationally justify, magically, intuitively flow into our minds, all because we had a time of youth, a time for gathering. Intuition is what 100 billion brain cells can do for you in their constant, natural, astonishing organizing. No computer comes close. No achievement test can measure it.

Despite its fundamental role in all of our mental, spiritual and, ultimately, professional development, few educators pay the slightest attention to this intuition and it was not mentioned in graduate schools of education, at least not in the eight years I studied in them. Rudolf Steiner, mystic and founder of Waldorf Schools, postulated that intuition is the third of three stages of higher knowledge, coming after imagination and inspiration, and that it is characterized by a state of immediate and complete experience of or union with knowledge. Intuition feeds upon our direct experience in the world—like a child, it needs exercise.

A 2009 report by the Alliance for Childhood surveyed kindergartens in New York City and Los Angeles and found that children had less than 30 minutes a day, on average, of "choice" time in which to do whatever they wanted. Then factor in that 40 percent of elementary schools in the U.S. reduced break-time between 1984 and 2004 as a way of addressing testing needs (Pappas 2011). In short, the race is on to exile the human intuition and to replace it with programmable, technology-driven and testable outcomes, often underneath fluorescent lighting and in stiff-backed chairs.

Of course, modern technology drives wealth creation and the promise of great benefits for us all. And, of course, wealth creation is not specifically what should be worrying us all. What should be of worrying us all is the accelerating and ironical presumption that we could never survive without all this technology.

All of this, and much more, is why I wanted a circle of tree stumps in the wildlife corridor behind our school. I wanted a space where, as Sugata Mitra phrased it, we could "Let children wander aimlessly around ideas."

It was mid-summer at the time. We were just starting some construction work and our construction foreman walked into my office carrying a sprig of Torrey pine tree needles. He had a dour look on his face. "It has to go," he said.

What he meant was the campus expansion necessitated the removal of an exquisite Torrey pine tree that I had planted 12 years ago right at the gateway of our school, at the very edge of the natural space by our school. We loved that tree. "It's not going," I replied. Not a question. "I'll be hugging it when the tree service comes. They'll have to take me with it." I wasn't going to let it go.

"It's going," he said. "If you want your campus finished, it's going. The water district needs to build in their gear in that space."

We walked around front and stood before the condemned tree. The Torrey pine tree only grows in this part of the world. I wasn't even sure if it was legal for us to cut it. It was quietly alive, like an elder. It whispered. It was bigger than I remembered. Stronger. The bottom was almost two feet across in diameter. The foreman just stood there, not bailing me out, not apologizing, not complicating anything, not moving or talking, just waiting for me. What a great teacher.

"When the tree service comes to take it down," I asked, "can they make stumps for us to sit on?" But it wasn't a real question. "Slices of about 15 inches each, for seats?"

The foreman surveyed the tree up and down: "It looks like

you could get about eight or nine good stumps out of it before it thins out up above."

Today, there is a circle of native tree stumps that we have returned back to the woods behind the school, and people go there for conversation and song, or just to sit. A young Torrey pine tree is planted next to it for shade. Someday it will grow to 70 feet tall.

Two UNESCO-Associate Schools exchange: Students from California and Weruweru School, Tanazania, processing some big questions

"Life is really simple, but we insist on making it complicated."
—Confucius

What Do We Care About?

Is there a difference between Eastern and Western purposes for schooling? As the east and the west emulate each other, what is lost?

After a tofu rice bowl lunch in my office, I had asked our two visiting Chinese teachers the simplest question I could think of: "As the head of the school, what do you think I care most about?" These teachers were among a group of eight who were hand-picked to come and observe western education and western values. We had already exchanged gifts in the oriental way, they giving me beautifully wrapped, aromatic teas and me quickly grabbing two school logo coffee cups to give in return. Coffee for tea.

The first teacher responded fairly quickly, "To boost international student enrollment." It was an intelligent answer. She had graduated in the top 3% of her high school class, graduated from a prestigious university, and now had a coveted job as a teacher of English language at a high school in the desirable Jiangsu Provence. The second visiting teacher did not find the question so simple. Considerable discussion ensued between the two in Chinese and I offered various framings of the question to help out: "What is valuable to me?" "What is the best thing that can happen at the school?"

The second teacher busied herself with her electronic translator and swapped ideas with the first teacher, then dug back into the translator, while scribbling some things on a pad of paper.

"What do we care most about?" I added, still prompting her.

At last, she responded, "Comprehensive quality of all courses in the school."

Good answer I thought before moving on to another area of discussion. Back home they were proud to be westernizing their schools by instituting some Advanced Placement (A.P.) exams for willing students as a way of replacing the famously grueling Gaokao National Examination System. So I asked, "What good does it do to replace one standardized exam with another? The A.P. is the least American educational program I know of!" I knew I would probably only confuse their thinking. To them, the A.P. was as American as cowboys.

They looked up from their notepads and e-translators. "Well, then, what do you care most about?" asked the first teacher. "Were we right?"

They looked at me gravely as though I were giving away a national security secret. "I just want our students to be happy," I revealed.

"I was going to guess that next," our visitor said, smiling.

Panamanian girls beneath their school on stilts, behind the mangroves.

"When you fight against something long enough, eventually you become the force you were fighting."

—Elina Lampert-Shepel

Boulder

If people are essentially self-interested, can they have a global perspective? Is the teacher's job more essentially to talk or to listen?

Deb Meier once said, maybe just to be shocking, that the purpose of education is to prepare people for being in the privileged class. Most likely, she was referring to the underserved, underprivileged, underclass. But for many, growing up in a caste of privilege is often a source of confusion. Despite being an object of aspiration for billions, many privileged youths haven't a clue about what to do with all that liberation.

The annual International Democratic Education Conference (the IDEC) switches nations every year and, in 2013, it was held in Boulder, Colorado. The group was diverse and the agendas were thick. Job titles listed on some of the business cards floating around included: Partnership for Change, Feminist Teacher, Humane Educator, Nuestra Escuela, Coming out of Silence and Changing the World, and Global Village School.

At one of the sessions, the moderator began with asking each of us to introduce ourselves by stating the pronoun we wished others to refer to us by. We started around the circle, one man offered up "he," but other answers included "she," "we," "they," and "you." One person wanted to be known as (from Rastafari) "I and I." There is a new, fluid, post-types world. In Colorado that summer, pot was about to be legalized, and on the expansive University of Colorado campus, a Ph.D. brain researcher was dropping acid after the sessions, while down at the river park people were chanting and strumming and selling granola mixes.

On the last day of the gathering, Sugata Mitra, the celebrated global educator and advocate for youth and their innate sense of wonder and wisdom, was seated in a tight circle of chairs with four other educators and community organizers, all of whom intended to tell their stories. This was striking because, Mitra, whose TED Talk featured on YouTube was approaching two million views, would clearly have keynoted at almost any educational conference in the world. Just that past February, he had won a $1 million prize from TED to advance his work, and yet at IDEC his name appeared in the conference program brochure in small print on a single page along with over 60 other conference presenters.

One chair was left empty in this inner circle, so that anyone in attendance could move in and have their say if they felt so compelled. Maybe a hundred, less than a fifth of the conference's 500 attendees, convened, all in three concentric circles around the center chairs. This is an educational methodology known as "the evolving fishbowl." But most people were really there just to see Mitra. The moderator, a Massachusetts college professor of education, welcomed all and passed the mic to his left. Mitra was on his right. As the mic circulated around, here is what came out of the fishbowl:

An organizer from Tennessee described the total "annihilation" of the public schools in her state. She said we needed a new collective liberation movement since the Tea Party had routed the teachers unions.

The next woman introduced herself as "white, straight, middle class." She detailed, however, that she was married to an Hispanic and makes sure every day to share in the advantages of her white privilege.

The mic was passed to the next person. It was "I and I," who said, "I feel like where we are, we need equity and dignity for the underprivileged who are disenfranchised." Then she ("I and I") proceeded to give details. Another person took the mic, and from all appearances she was coming from that place of white privilege, and she expressed the sense of marginalization she experienced here in Boulder, suddenly a member of a small and little-represented minority. How unusual this was given her background. Was this the marginalization of privilege? Could it be that disenfranchisement comes from being in any class, however high or low?

Sugata Mitra at last got the mic. He spoke about how people could get the basic skills from school that the workforce needs by the age of 10. After that, the best schools could do, would be to leave the students alone and respect their innate curiosity. He added that our standard curricular programming of academic skills and content was largely meaningless and of little value to 90% of families in the world since their largest hope is finding any kind of work whatsoever.

A new woman moved quickly into the center and took the empty chair. She introduced herself as a black woman of privilege and felt curriculum should be like after-school programs where kids are more free.

Someone else moved into the center and sat in the empty chair. She said the government is only concerned with pleasing industry and large corporations and added, by contrast, that really we all share a lot in common.

Then a person outside the circle was handed a microphone and explained that we must live peace and truly be peace.

A Chinese educational researcher got into the inner circle and, standing and nodding her head vigorously, detailed how the government in China tries to control the people, such as censoring feminist writings including (and by now she was screaming) some of her own. If we create new sources of media we can create a new society, she concluded.

The conversation spiraled as a wild subtext emerged on the complexities and frustrations inherent in participatory democracy. After a couple of more statements from the inner circle, a woman in the back row said she was sorry if this was a change of subject, but that many of us were there to hear Dr. Mitra and could he please be given the mic. (I said to myself, "Yeah!")

Sugata Mitra exlained there are four billion parents in the world and what they want was for their children to be able to get or create jobs.

Focusing on his words didn't last long though as someone from Detroit said their schools had 75 pupils in a class, that students were suspended for 4 days if they didn't have their ID, and that students go to jail for minor school infractions. It was the school-to-prison pipeline. And she added, why must only poor schools get young Teach for America privileged kids who displace real teachers and then leave in two years?

Then two or three more people spoke about the privileges of oppressors in American schooling. All these shades of shame—where was the light?

"I don't know about being an oppressor," the only teenager in the room jumped up to say. He was a skinny, sandy blonde kid from Southern California. "I feel like I'm a lucky, privileged person without much to show for it. I have no idea what I'm supposed to do, I don't feel particularly special, and yet I have about as good a life as anyone could ask for. Perhaps the best word to describe being me is *khaki*—like a pair of khaki pants, my life feels sort of bland, ordinary—and yet functional, objectively pretty comfortable. I suppose this isn't a bad thing, but as a teenager I don't really know where I'm at or where I'm supposed to be at. Adolescence is weird, and the way it feels to be me right here right now matches that." Was it conceivable that this surf kid, this trespasser, was expressing the aspirations of almost everyone in the room?

And could he know marginalization worthy of the attentions of the "real" disenfranchised? And when we are at last awakened from own social milieu and despair, will we find a much larger real world, dark and unfixable? Is this the "privilege" education must prepare us all for?

Finally, the moderator took the floor and said there was only one minute left in the session and, aware of the elephant in the room, handed the mic back to Mitra. How could he possibly conclude this session strangely labeled "Media, Arts and Democratic Education"? Could he, in one minute, turn this venting session into a legitimate conversation?

"I have heard about all these problems before," he explained. "You are talking about 300 million people in the United States. And there are 6.8 billion people in the rest of the world who don't give a sh*t about any of this." Suddenly, as though a buzzer had ended class, the minorities were all transmogrified and there were only humans in all their colors, standing up, shuffling around in silence or whispering, taking their leave. Mitra looked up with a cherubic grin and said to somebody, "I couldn't resist."

All over the world students face standardization of their educational programming. Author in Cuban school.

"A merry heart doeth good like a medicine; but a broken spirit drieth the bones"

—Book of Proverbs, 17:22

Han
(Happiness as a Measurable Educational Outcome)

What if we assigned, benchmarked, taught, and measured student happiness in school: Graded it, paid teachers for it, and ranked school systems by it?

Koreans, anthropologically, must be part Chinese and part oceanic, and their world-class work ethic and studiousness is balanced with warm-heartedness and graciousness as though they are permanently engaged in resolving some timeless human riddle.

In large, bureaucratic schools, the Koreans have pursued high test scores unsparingly and with success which has turned them into leaders in the global education competition. Why then would they fly me, a progressive small schools advocate from a nation ranked well below their own, to their land to address a goal as lofty, elusive and globally ineffable as, "cultivating dreams for happiness in education?"

As young teachers in the 1970s and 80s, Korean education had always been our hyperbole for overcrowded and pressured classes, but we are well into a new millennium now. At present, Korean schools are rated at or near the top of the world among nations. Another profound change since my early career days occurred to me: Back then, only a sell-out teacher would actually "teach to the test," but now they universally feel required to. After a generation of devotion to high test scores,

Korea's educational success had evidently taken them to a place where few nations historically have ever been able to go: the serious consideration of how to become happy. That year's conference, a concept that may have been unfathomable only a generation ago, was entitled: "International Perspectives on Happiness Education." As an emerging science, we now can test for student happiness almost the same way we can test for knowledge of algebra. But, of course, we do not.

The journey to Korea, from California, across the international date line, is long enough to be transformational. On long plane rides, I have learned to adopt slug-like contortions and meld into a semi-dream state for hours at a time. Exhausted and exercise-deprived from 20 hours of incarceration in the tiny compartment of the Boeing 737, I wound around the hallways of Icheon Airport. Was it exercise or sleep my body was asking for? I had no words to describe this in-between state I arrived in, but eventually I learned one.

I was met at the airport by a grinning first-year teacher and a Ph.D. educational researcher. With barely time for a change of clothing and stretching my body back into shape, we headed straight for dinner and seated ourselves on the floor around a traditional table over a Korean sizzling wok and three kinds of kimchi, Korea's take on pickles. There we were joined by the 10 organizers and teachers involved in that year's Seoul annual conference including a senior researcher from Seoul National University's Center for Happiness. My legs seized up under the table as my fingers wrestled with the skinny, metal chopsticks.

I asked my new friends what their problems were in helping students be happier. Their answer should have been no surprise. It was the same answer I received when I asked similar questions of parents of high performing Chinese students. It was the answer I got from my Cuban tour guide as we visited Havana schools, from a friend who teachers in a desolate, post-industrial mining town in Wales, from international educators at University of Alicante, Spain, and from teachers from all around the world whom I had met at the International Democratic Education Conference the previous summer. It was the same answer I hear repeatedly from teachers from schools I accredit across the American Southwest, from the physics teacher I met from Arusha in Tanzania, and from a teacher in south central L.A. who quit the profession this year. I hear this answer from progressive teachers, conservative teachers, teachers who are fresh and starting out, and teachers who are fed up. Their answer was the same as that from pretty much every single teacher in every forum in which I have taken part in the last several years. And that answer was, in the developed world, teachers feel penalized for curriculum they are supposed to cover in a year but can't get to in time. Add to this, they feel demoralized that their worth and fate as professionals are determined by the standardized test scores their students get at the end of each year they spend in this race.

So, I listened as teachers once again explained this globally repressed sentiment. Millennial educators and parents widely view themselves in a "race to nowhere." Around the wok, I learned that in submitting to this global reality, Korean teens get six hours of sleep a night, not enough to develop or nurture qualities like empathy and creativity, much less happiness. Many sleep with their cellphone standing by, further diminishing the quality of what rest they get. Their homework load leaves virtually no time for free play or time in nature, much less time for enough sleep. For teens, dreaming is no longer the province of night.

Earlier in 2013 in Seoul at her swearing in to office, following a merry ceremony featuring a 21-gun salute, dancers, and Psy giving it up Gangnam Style, Park Geun-hye, South Korea's new president, made a revolutionary promise—to make her workaholic, ultra-competitive, stressed out people happy: "I will usher in a new era of hope, whereby the happiness of each citizen becomes the bedrock of our nation's strength," she proclaimed. This goal quickly flowed into the national ministries, including the Seoul Ministry of Education.

Though scarcely a prayer for somewhere between six and seven billion of the world's people, happiness was becoming the minor fascination spreading around the developed world. Seoul's courage to focus on happiness as a real goal is a leadership vision that sees far beyond the stellar standardized test results of its sleep-deprived students. "Beware the barrenness of the busy life," Socrates is said to have warned.

The conference began the next day at the beautiful Millennium Hilton. The forum was opened by Dr. Yonglin Moon, Superintendent of the Seoul Office of Education, who cited research from Seoul's National University's Happiness Research Center that happy teachers make happy students. He urged, "Let's help our teachers to boost their pride and professionalism, so that they lead our students with love and devotion."

Pride. Love. Devotion . . . The list of core values espoused by schools as outcomes for their graduates was an inspiration. So many lofty goals. Our students will be leaders. Our students will excel. Our students will persevere. Our students will be characterized by fine traits: Compassion. Collaboration. Gratitude. Love. Happiness!

Despite all these ideals though, when teachers are evaluated annually, world over, they are still judged fundamentally by how far they have progressed in the race to complete the year's requirements, along with a small handful of test scores and perhaps grade point averages. Likewise, the overall careers of teachers, however deeply bound they become in the developing lives of their students, are determined by these same, one-dimensional scores. Not happiness.

In delivering his congratulatory opening, Dr. Moon was doing more than waxing positive. Psychologists have repeatedly associated happiness with all sorts of attributes that would help schools, including strong immune systems, higher job satisfaction levels for teachers and supervisors, and various other aspects of optimal human functioning.

Nations too are tiered in the same way teachers are. Despite Korea's rank as one of the top two nations in the world in academic test taking (Pearson, 2013), the nation has been found to score 63rd among 151 nations tested on the Happy Planet Index (New Economics Foundation, 2013). So, President Park had her work cut out for herself, as did Dr. Moon. Given this goal, it is inspiring to think what South Korea could have been accomplishing if its students were not only high achieving, but happy as well.

At lunch after the conference opening, I was seated by Dr. Moon, I with an open collar sport shirt and he in formal business attire. I was puzzled now at my role, on the one hand wanting to respect local mores and on the other hand wanting to earn my consulting pay, and so I queried, as scientifically as possible, "If we are serious about happiness as an educational outcome for our children, why don't we measure it and evaluate our teachers on this in addition to the academic scores of their students?"

Dr. Moon said nothing. The Satisfaction with Life Scale (SWLS), the Positive and Negative Affect Schedule (PANAS), and the Subjective Happiness Scale (Seoul International Education Forum, 2013) are just a few of the happiness batteries available. The energy and dedication it takes to achieve Korea's current rating is astonishing, and yet high test scores are primarily an indicator of how well students are prepared for what is on those tests, and relatively little else. And does no one care that the report on global rankings of national school systems was published by Pearson, the test publication corporation now earning billions of dollars each year from this rat race? Pressing on just a bit, I bid Dr. Moon to just imagine if Korea, with all of its concentration and resolution, were to set its testing sights on something grander such as a synthesis of happiness and high achievement. "And what about measuring and ranking our other educational values like kindness, integrity, and curiosity, so that teachers could be supported in addressing them?"

Dr. Moon gave me a quick and dignified glance that I found alarming. I had no words or concepts to interpret this in-between look. What dozens of new questions did my singular question trigger? Had I opened a door to some intercultural abyss?

"How can they dream if they don't sleep?" I pleaded, feeling lost and doubtful that such a metaphor could even translate. Dr. Moon changed the subject.

The next evening at dinner on the bank of the River Han, we prepared for our goodbyes. There, looking out across the water, white, yellow and purple lights bleeding into the calm blackness of the wide expanse, full moon above, I learned of the ancient concept of *han*, an untranslatable belief that is said to sum up the unique Korean spirit. Han is the space between our eternal desires and the realities we can never quite accept. Han is the beauty at the very tip of our tongue we might barely taste but never possess. It is the deep longing that always lies just beyond our grasp. Han is the way the best of the world's teachers view the happiness of their students, or their very jobs.

Han is the knowledge that, if any nation were to judge its teachers based upon the results of their students in academic skills and happiness combined, this would be an historic step, a step of unprecedented courage and kindness. Those teachers would have grounds for gratitude and would surely earn the attention of the world.

After the conference, a top-level educational researcher escorted me to the airport. Could Korea ever risk its educational rankings and squarely face the inopportune realities of sleep deprived, nature deprived, play deprived kids trapped in an ever-expanding, centralized educational bureaucracy? The researcher thought not any time soon, but that the vision is there for the teachers. Han. "At lunch ...he was not listening to you," the researcher said.

School day, Bocas del Toro, Panama.

"It's quite fashionable to say that the educational system is broken. It's not broken. It's wonderfully constructed. It's just that we don't need it anymore."

—Sugata Mitra

Education in the *Real World*

What presumptions about "normal" schools are holding us back?

❝ If the school is very small, how will it prepare students for the *real world*?" a Korean reporter asked. We wondered aloud if her "real world" job entailed sitting in rows all day long in groups of 40 or so people who were made to follow explicit instructions by managers who would be judged by the scores their staff received on a test at the end of the year.

This *real world* often seems to be invoked by people who are fearful of change. They often see education as a system we process kids through to achieve standard, reliable results. It's the race to the cubicle.

Here is the real world as some students know it: guys stealing lunch money; students slouching in the back rows of history class; a basketball jock hocking a loogie at an oil painting in the office foyer; stressed out over-achievers who measure their worth by their scores and rank in school. But who can conceive of a real world that includes our elders as teachers, an education in natural green spaces, and students gathered around in groups just big enough to have deepening conversations?

Studies are filled with beautiful, stirring examples of those who have bailed on the real world . . . and in so doing, found it. In 2003, Orchard Gardens Pilot School in Massachusetts, nearly 100 percent black and Hispanic, opened its doors with a posse of security guards to ensure the campus was under tight controls. Backpacks were prohibited for fear of weapons and discipline issues were rampant, including violence. In 2010, a new principal, Andrew Bott, came in, threw out the security guards and put the money into art teachers. As a result, student achievement grew faster than anywhere in the state, vandalism subsided, and student expression blossomed.

Fearless educators, such as those in small and community-based schools like Orchard Gardens, are open to new realities as they emerge. Despite a real world of teacher control and domination, research makes it clear that teachers whom students perceive as highly effective see their purposes as freeing rather than controlling. These same teachers view people as friendly rather than unfriendly. They see people, and especially their students, as worthy. Students feel connected to teachers like this. And, subsequently to higher causes which they pursue, taking them beyond just the classroom. This sounds like the real world.

In a couple years, Bott got a plum assignment in a prime, Boston suburb, and left the inner city.

Author with the Korean minister of education, 2014.

"The work of Warriors is to remember who we are as humans and to make it possible for many people to rediscover how it feels to be fully human. We plunge open-hearted into this world of confusion, aggression and greed, inviting challenge, practicing discernment, accepting change and uncertainty, coping with despair and exhaustion. And from it all we find rich lives overflowing with meaning and delight because the human spirit is always worth working for."

—Margaret Wheatley

What the Revolution Looks Like

When was the last time you had a great conversation with a teen? To what extent do teachers risk their jobs to do this? Would you risk a job as a teacher in pursuit of great conversations?

One of the opening workshops at the Alternative Educators Resource Organization (AERO) annual conference one year, held at C.W. Post College of Long Island University in beautiful, green Brookville was entitled, "Loving Them into Being." Alternative educators in our field are pre-occupied with ensuring that teaching entails the most basic things imaginable: listening to and caring for our students, giving students a voice, giving them honest and timely evaluations, making time for play and joy, creating the conditions for collaboration, and creating school environments that feel safe.

In California, where I live, "alternative education" has a bad name. Somehow, it got the connotation as "schools for kids who can't make it." The state of alternative education is that it's a field where a prominent, committed and passionate network of innovators and scholars are also widely presumed not to be doing anything of general utility. Some of our most enlightened educators are invisibly functioning primarily for the benefit of the marginalized, the failing, the disenfranchised, and the needlessly creative.

One of the workshops at AERO that year was called, "An Outsider's Perspective." The mission of AERO is that "learner-centered education will become available for all students." Is that the revolution? "That makes sense from an outsider's perspective," said one attendee. She was new to AERO, and nobody knew if she was an outsider here and an insider in the mainstream, or vice versa, and she didn't know either.

In America, alternative educational structures began to increase in the first part of the new millennium: home schooling, themed charter schools, homeschool resource centers, independent schools (the original and oldest form of schooling in the nation), free schools, democratic schools, and hybrids. Angela Kost, an AERO presenter, noted, "the inherent strengths of the homeschool model are what we should be striving for in public school." Like her workshop, entitled, "Founding a Public Unschool," many of the other conference sessions had the tinge of revolution about them such as "Building the Movements," or "The Evils of Bureaucratic Public Education" and "Enhancing Student Freedom."

The relationship between public and alternative education was being hotly debated at this AERO gathering. Basic conflicts were at play. Like free will versus authority and open space versus closed space. As a further example, Professor Elina Lampert-Shepel lectured on the compassionate Vygotsky model, which is big in Russia and Brazil. It calls for temperance as we organize against the U.S. educational model that she described as "totalitarian." She cautioned, "When you fight against something long enough, eventually you become the force you were fighting," reminding us all to keep watching our backs. Then keynote speaker Peter Gray went on to declare the U.S. public school system nationwide is "beyond redemption." On the last night, North Star founder and *Huffington Post* blogger Ken Danforth spoke of his motto, "School is optional." Holding his manifesto, *The Teenage Liberation Handbook* by Grace Llewellyn, up before the audience, he mused about a revolution where all U.S. families would rise up and file for homeschooling and the entire public school system would collapse like an old barn.

Movements are underway to get legitimate life preparation outside of the university as well. For example, go on the Internet and check out Mycelium School, Experience Institute, Geronimo School, Enstitute, Nomads, and Teale Institute—all knowledge-creation organizations you do not need $30,000 a year to enroll in. Free "massive open online courses" (MOOC) had thousands, which have turned into millions, of "outside" students virtually sitting in on lectures by notable professors at Stanford and elsewhere. MOOC universities or, more accurately, gathering centers, are popping up for these outsiders to gather and share, and apply self-organizing principals to create unschooling campuses. Maybe any place with an Internet connection is a one-room schoolhouse.

To the alternative educator, public schooling may always appear pre-occupied with ensuring that each school is a compliant part of huge bureaucracies. Due largely to the growing expense of these bureaucracies, alternative, small schools—those with less than 230 students and even schools within schools of up to 400 students—are often no more costly than what large, urban districts are budgeted for.

By 2015 in America, we had worked our way up to a $60 billion a year federal department of education with primary contractors being global corporations. They all claim they are reformers. For example, Pearson is paid billions to administer standardized tests that benchmark students and teachers. According to the National Center for Educational Statistics, the ranks of non-teachers—such as administrators, counselors, teacher aides and cafeteria workers—has swelled 130 percent since 1970 and they now make up 50 percent of all public school employees. Deep inside these big systems, about a third of all high school kids claim they feel sad or hopeless. Alternative educators wanted no part of that money, any more than they wanted a part of the hopelessness.

The truth is, AERO didn't feel like a revolution to me. It just felt like regular people searching for connection. I packed my bags, folded up my brand new "Education Revolution" tee shirt and thought perhaps, hopefully, an emerging vision holds more opportunities for entrepreneurial and intrinsic learning. Maybe the "revolution" is really just about encouraging natural curiosity. If we had the will, we could free children from the gigantic systems we've turned schooling into and invite them into learning communities where their "inner" voices could come "out."

When I got home, walking my dog in the neighborhood green, a five-year old I knew was on all fours and completely absorbed in something. As I approached, he looked up. "Worms are cool," he said. Could this be what the revolution looks like?

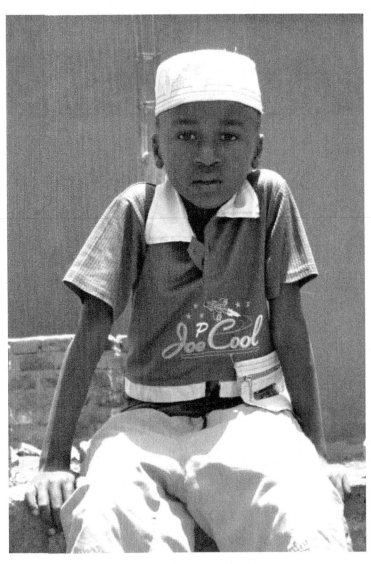

What if there are no answers? Can we live with these questions?

"Sorrow everywhere. Slaughter everywhere. If babies are not starving someplace, they are starving somewhere else. With flies in their nostrils. But we enjoy our lives because that's what God wants."

—Jack Gilbert

Find Your People

What are we doing to give our students a sense of real belongingness in the classroom and around the campuses of America? Is the teacher's fundamental allegiance to the school system . . . or to their students?

So, I was in the country, logging country, and on my way to a consultation with a small, independent school that needed some encouragement. It was a small town not far from the foot of Mount St. Helens.

In Washington state, the coffee shop is the town hall so I was off to the first meeting in a tiny coffee house. I introduced myself to the faculty. There were six of them. The teachers had no agenda, but they did have curiosity. And they loved their kids and their kids loved them. How wonderful to find a school where the teachers exuded openness like that.

The second meeting was at a Starbucks, where I met a small group of parents. They were thankful. Their school, named the Family House School, was independent, small, inclusive, personalized and they loved it. Such a beautiful school, and so simple: students and teachers in a ranch house at the edge of the damp, green, shadowy forest, talking about big values and really listening to one another. It was a school that dared to have a sense of place. Every day started out with a meeting of the whole, grades kindergarten through ninth grade packed together. No big-stakes tests, no curriculum standards set from

3,000 miles away. Every day, the leader shared stories evoking the natural power of tribal gathering. Parents could even join right in in the classroom and no one minded.

But still, not only there in Washington but nationwide, it can be a real struggle getting communities to understand how legitimate an alternative school is, even if their kids are happier there. Communities feel enormous pressure to comply with the prevalent, comprehensive school model, even though a majority of people don't like it. Communities also seem generally unaware of how possible it really is to have teacher/student relationships as the basis of schooling, how essential that is, and how rare that has become. So lost this once-obvious concept has become in our schools that many communities or school boards hardly remember or conceive of it as a possibility. So Family House was facing this problem.

The school was neither faith-based nor hippy-based. Classes are calm and focused with a balance of tolerance and obedience and an emphasis on responsibility and respect. It would appeal to diverse parents, whether liberal or conservative, and there were plenty of both—but it was small and simple. Things schools have long forgotten, such as age-mixing and presuming kids to have various learning styles—no labels—are normal again here. Everyone is supported by everyone. Teachers routinely invite student reflection. Students typically refer to their school using phrases like: "A place where I belong," and "an indiscriminating environment where you learn to be tolerant of all kinds of kids." In America, when we peer into a school and find happy or free kids, or when a visionary leader is present, our suspicions are quickly aroused. With both in evidence, Family House was presumed by some to be unreliable and amateurish.

The third meeting was at a medium-sized coffee house, with two public school teachers. I had no idea why they were even interested in Family House. But before long I began to learn why. As talk grew deeper, one of them asked, "How can I channel my anger against the system?" I recognized these feelings from educators in large, comprehensive schools not just from around our country, but from around the world, particularly among secondary school teachers. Systems are getting bigger. Strong, dark emotions are welling up in this new world and none of this has been covered in teacher training. It's new territory. After dinner, these teachers agonized for an hour and a half. "I don't know what to do with these emotions—I keep coming back to this sense of rage against our school administration or our government, and I know this isn't going to get better—the system doesn't support me. But I want to stay in this struggle."

And there it was. "The system doesn't support me."

I know this is not exclusive to education. It happens wherever systems replace people: in law, health care, corporate life, social services. In athletics and in governments.

There is so much despair wherever we look. Can we really pretend this will get better? I have almost never met a person from a current, large comprehensive, secondary school system who feels that either things are getting better, that enlightened people will arrive, or money will flow in, and somehow save them. The systems required to hold all this together are growing faster than the systems they are set up to serve. We can try righteous anger but righteous anger does nothing. People either dislike the system, or they take it on faith that this is the way things are supposed to be. The thought that "we can rise up against this, we can fix this," is the very falsehood that prevents facing what is. "Humans have always risen up in the past," or so goes some thought, which is also false. "We'll create technology," some people love to claim too with their "Magical Thinking." And this is false. Here is the way it is: This system is not getting better. It is not going to get better.

We can cruise along imagining blissfulness and being

avoidant, or we can make some decisions. As teachers, do we leave a corrupt system or just close our classroom door and pretend to ignore it? As teachers, do we just insist that our work matters, smile and press on knowing that things are falling apart? *The systems required to hold all this together are growing faster than the systems they are set up to serve.* And what if there are no answers? Can we live with these questions?

"You have to be willing to risk your job and reputation—either that, or stop complaining," I say to these teachers in the coffee shop. Maybe that's cruel of me to suggest.

"I just close the door," answered one of them, world-weary from overcrowded classes, relentless hurrying, and the ceaseless specter of judgment. So we close the classroom door. We close out evil, fear and hope, and in there we can have open space and some tiny pocket of freedom, which is our very own. It is the new millennium resignation: resign but stay in the job. These two teachers felt spurned. They can close the classroom door and live in this separateness from their communities. Inside, perhaps there will even be a pocket of wonderment, however hidden away from the system it is. "If we deny our happiness, resist our satisfaction, we lessen the importance of their deprivation," said the poet Jack Gilbert. Happiness can be our weapon. Perhaps we can at least permit our own, sequestered joy.

Not far from where I was visiting, the University of Washington had created "The Center for Reinventing Public Education," perhaps evidence of awakening. But does anyone in the whole world really think this all will be fixed? Does anyone think the din of craving or distraction will just stop, like God putting noise-canceling headphones on the world? (And aren't a million teens already doing this?) Who are we kidding? Closing the door was the only way these two teachers, and millions like them, could abide in their real work, and find a little space for their craft.

"When an old culture is dying," noted Rudolf Bahro, "a new culture is born from a few people willing to be embarrassed." Talking about self-respect and freedom in education felt like sticking our necks out for many of us during quite a few years. Places like Family House have weathered the storms. For their part, the people in Family House are good teachers. They mainly wanted to know of their work: "Is this okay?" "Can I persevere?" Especially the founder who wrote later, "I'm really looking hard at the realization that I can't continue to work the 60+ hours each week."

Perhaps it is humiliation or exhaustion that drives teachers over the edge, to the point where they can no longer even close the door and do real work. Maybe they leave the profession. If it's not too late, typically meaning if they have taught less than four years or so, some go to places like Family House to teach. Maybe this is what *reinventing* really looks like.

I could drink no more coffee, and we parted. The next day I spent inside the classrooms of Family House, sunk into a zone where the local sense of place is a fundamental part of the school day and a national curriculum seems foreign. It is a zone where art is inseparable from any other academic discipline, a zone where there is time for finishing what we start, a zone where age difference is not a divider of children but an opportunity for mentoring. And now my observations are complete.

Somewhere it was decided that I would present my observations to the whole and I was given directions to another coffee house. I arrived at the huge building, equal in size to any 10 Starbucks I have ever seen. A sign on the door read, "ATTENTION: Out of respect for tonight's speaker, we will stop serving coffee at 6:30 PM." Wow—this was a big deal. No coffee served. At any rate, no coffee after 6:30 was a good thing. It was already going to take me a week to get rid of the jitters I had from a week of coffee houses.

I entered and saw tables and chairs for well over 100 people, which were filling up quickly, plus standing room. They were all there to honor the brave, little independent school, both anachronistic and futuristic in ways anyone would want a school to be: caring and doing no harm, warm, intensely connected, not solving global problems, not making promises, simply acting well in their work. Doing the right thing.

In the corner was a large stage with rock band gear pushed to the back, and a spotlight was ready on a tall café table and chair, center stage.

By now I had switched to chai (no caffeine). I took a sip and reflected before the tribe. Just that month in American education:

"A handful of schools across the country are banning homework

"The American Academy of Pediatrics is sounding the alarm on epidemic levels of sleep deprivation among teens

"The movie *Race To Nowhere*, which launched five years ago at The Grauer School, is still showing in 30 locations nationwide

"Hundreds of students poured out of at least five Jefferson County, Colorado schools to protest what they say is the Jeffco School Board's attempt to whitewash history."

I explained, "On the Indian reservations they are rebuilding their native languages. Small towns all over the country are saying no to school consolidation, and saying yes to smaller, inclusive, safer schools with local controls." More people clapped. We shared stories about small schools and the successes in this very town's own small school all week—a school with the audacity to call itself Family House. When you are out there, doing a separate thing, following your heart, sometimes you wonder how crazy you might be, and at those times it's reassuring to check in with someone you trust, almost like getting permission from the big guys upstairs. So you can keep doing it.

Some people clapped at the notion that local communities are "taking it back." This phenomenon, "taking it back," is not partisan or regional. It is happening in places where people fly the American flag off their pickup trucks, and I see it just as well in my home town of Encinitas, Southern California, where the cars are loaded up with surfboards. People want it back, whatever it is.

"You are a part of a network that spans the globe," I pointed out. "Americans are standing up against authoritarian control over local schooling. Small, place-based schools are not less by virtue of size. They are safer, higher achieving and more connected. They may feel alone, but they are a part of the Small Schools Coalition, Progressive Educators Network, Community Works Institute, the Coalition of Essential Schools, and Alternative Educators Resource Organization among others. A school may feel isolated out there in the country, but in reality, it is connected to an international network, bonded by the single-most important concept we will ever need to know about schooling.

"The research says what we already knew, that people are not only happiest, but most productive when they are with people they care about. A great teacher understands that engagement is not primarily about the subjects studied or the required curriculum and testing—it is about the relationships that are forming in the class. Connection . . . is the single most important thing in all of pedagogy. Find your people and make them your school."

So that was it. 150 people clapping that they did not need to be faceless members lost in a system. This can be our own school. Our own culture. Our own vision. Our own community.

We do not need to stay in this mess. Humans have the extraordinary capacity for delight with one another, and all good things may come if we merely try to reclaim that, however small it is. What if our goals include a few moments of bliss now and then, no matter what else is going on?

Amidst the clapping, it was easy to be taken in by my own ego, and I understand that this has been the downfall of change-makers more impactful than me. But, for an egotistical minute, the allure was undeniable. It's just fantastic that as soon as we let go of our despair and think we are home free, we can jump right into egocentrism. Maybe they are flip sides of the same thing.

I cut out of there, hungry and a long way from my flight in Seattle. Driving north, the radio said, "Mount St. Helens is showing signs of reawakening." Wow. I pulled into a burger joint and got distracted photographing pheasants that were penned into the back of a farm truck. I loved how there would be absolutely nothing like this back where I was headed. I was talking to the driver, an elderly farmer dressed in dungaree coveralls who was on his way to release these birds into the wild in time for hunting season, peering into cages, when a projectile filled my eye and I started backwards and grabbed my face, blinking madly. The farmer knew . . .

"Whaddee flip a turd?" he asked, wry and knowing.

"I keep learning the hard way," I said back, trying to wipe the guacamole-like slime from my eye. "There is hope; though not for us," wrote Kafka, but he had no sense of humor. The point is, if we want to let go of despair and egocentrism, or even invite in a little comedy, no one can stop us in that, either. For teachers, I recommend it. I know things are hard, but we can press on.

"We are the Indians, The mighty, mighty Indians..."
—Manhasset High School Cheering Squad, 1968

"In our every deliberation, we must consider the impact of our decisions on the next seven generations."
—The Great Law of the Iroquois Confederacy

The Manhasset Indians
(Lacrosse and the Real History of Comprehensive Schools in America)

Does bussing work? 25 million American students now go on 10 million, socially questionable school bus trips per year. What could we get back if we had local community schools again? What are the unintended impacts of school consolidation?

The town of Manhasset, Long Island, where I grew up, was divided into two distinct sections: the high ground, where all the original, white-flight suburban settlements were, and a small outskirts called the "Valley." African-American families were settled down in the Valley, and they made up about 90% of the Valley population, along with a very few eastern and southern Europeans.

Manhasset is an American Indian name meaning "island neighborhood," but the Valley was not a part of the neighborhood. As a young boy, I rarely met an African-American and I'm pretty sure I never met an American Indian out there in the suburbs, either.

A neglected, rarely documented aspect of white-flight from the cities is that not all whites were the same, and suburban communities sprung up that were filled with heterogeneity, divisiveness, fear, and of course some elitism. Naturally, I rarely ventured down into the Valley. Once, though, at 13, I went with a small group to visit the Mount Olive Baptist Church and this was where I first learned of old time religion. This also was my first witnessing of a small, tribe-like community, passionate about its culture. There were kids I knew from junior high, like Jimmy and Ralph, singing and filled with pride. I would have loved to go to a school with kids of those families, except, of course, they were off the island. The church was like nothing I had ever seen in the "Strathmore" part of town. Down in the valley, they sang and prayed together like something out of the Bible and their primary school consisted of 160 students, a near perfect size historically for belongingness and a tribal sense of community.

A few years later, after I graduated high school and turned 18, I went back to the Valley from time to time to drop into the Hilltop Inn, incongruously perched at the edge of the Valley. There, an Irish barkeep called John Colamick kept a German shepherd named Duke. We played pool to pass the evenings and had a few beers and, whenever a black man opened the door to consider entering, Duke began uncontrollably barking while John made a terrible show of reining him in. Any black interloper would wisely close the door and John would reward Duke with some good kibble and pats on the back. "Good, Duke!"

So, growing up, I was aware of almost no integration between the two parts of town. The Valley School served the blacks, which provided elementary education for the children of our maids and blue collar workers. When I came of junior high age, I entered Manhasset Junior and Senior High where we (from Strathmore village) were thrown together with the kids from the other two small, tribe-like elementary schools, Plandome Road School (largely Catholic) and the Valley School (blacks). Manhasset High was the supposed melting pot, salad bowl, or what have you.

*****

Manhasset High was primarily famous for its lacrosse teams. Lacrosse was another connected community in our town. Like an Indian tribe of long ago, the Manhasset lacrosse team was able to summon a tribal inclusiveness and spirit that enabled its players to experience pride and connection, even as many other students, suddenly thrown together from the safe-feeling, inclusive schools of their elementary years, may have felt lost and threatened. High school sports teams continue to serve this tribal function as a workaround for the fact that growing numbers of students and teachers in our schools, which have grown steadily in size for well over 100 years, feel caught in the hierarchical control and command system of the modern comprehensive schools.

Football legend Jimmy Brown had attended Manhasset High just a few years before I had. Brown was bigger, faster and stronger than most every other athlete he would encounter at every level of sports. Though he ultimately became known as a pro football hall of famer, Manhasset became a lacrosse epicenter starting in Jimmy Brown's days due largely to his legendary talent. When intercepting any ball from his position at midfield, he merely clamped the lacrosse stick to his chest and barreled straight down field into the opposing goal, completely unstoppable. According to the Lacrosse Hall of Fame, they actually changed the rules of the game because of Brown. Now you need to cradle the stick away from your body so that someone can try to get at the ball. Jimmy Brown is still widely considered the greatest lacrosse player in the history of high school lacrosse. He of course grew up in the Valley, his mother was a maid and, for all I knew, she might have been cleaning my house during those years.

To this same effect, my earliest memory of the black kids I began encountering in junior high is that many of them towered over me and were powerful and alien. Early in eighth grade I entered the bathroom and this is where I met Jimmy

Jackson, in my grade but in none of my classes. Jimmy was almost a foot taller than I was. "Hey Grauer-man," he said, with a grin. "Hey, Jimmy," I said, and proceeded to the sink, not paying any attention. Before I knew it, he had grasped me with a giant hand, and was good-naturedly holding me out the open, second floor window. Looking back, my dangling situation was a fairly accurate depiction of my life as a teen in suburbia, and yet it had to have been even more descriptive of Jimmy's life than of my own. Either way, as I try to contemplate the weight of cultural and historical forces in play all leading up to that moment suspended out the bathroom window, it seems unfathomable. It's likely that his great-grandparents were slaves in Georgia or thereabouts (and before that perhaps a thousand years of tribal life deeply rooted in nature), while mine were either plundered or banished in the pogroms of Austria-Hungary; or, on the other side of my family, run out of England for religious persecution. What forces led us to meet in this place? Was it a culmination of something? There out the window, I beheld the school lacrosse field just across the quad, smiling frantically and imagining the broken bones I'd have if Jimmy let go. Just then, in walked Ralph Blocker.

Ralph was tall, broad shouldered, very handsome, had a movie star smile, and was black. "Jimmy, what are you doing?" Ralph protested. "You don't wanna throw Grauer out the window!" I suppose it was a good thing that Ralph had some sense of what was going on, because I surely didn't have a clue.

Jimmy thought for a second. "Aw, Ralph, I wouldn't do that to him," he answered. "That's m'boy!" And he pulled me in, still smiling.

I have a scant few memories of junior high school, and hardly an in-class memory that is vivid at all. I know I looked up to Ralph Blocker from then, on, though. Later on, in high school, he was the only black kid I ever knew to ask out a white girl, an Irish girl called Colleen who I didn't dare ask out. Now, exactly 50 years later, I have to wonder, was that moment in the boys room the moment something clicked in Ralph's mind, a small moment he somehow recognized as a seed of something larger, something you could forever look into like a prism? Was this what a paradigm really looks like when you're really in it? Though unfathomable to me at the time, that brief encounter was so purely crazy, yet so perfect, that maybe it was an invisible pivot point in education nationwide. It is actually possible . . .

A generation passed. It was the 1980s and I was researching multicultural education. There in the law library of the University of San Diego, I turned a page and was stunned to see this: "BLOCKER v. BOARD OF EDUCATION OF MANHASSET, NEW YORK NO. 62-C-285."

Ralph BLOCKER, a minor . . . et al., Plaintiffs, v. The BOARD OF EDUCATION OF MANHASSET, NEW YORK . . .

THE COMPLAINT

This is a class action instituted by several Negro minors who reside within Union Free School District No. 6, Manhasset, New York (the District), [**226 F.Supp. 209**] against The Board of Education of Manhasset, New York, its members and its Superintendent of Schools. The plaintiffs allege that they and the members of their class are discriminated against by the defendants by being racially segregated in the use and enjoyment of the public schools of the District; that the defendants are denying them their rights under the Fourteenth Amendment to the Constitution of the United States and the Civil Rights Act, 42 U.S.C. §§ 1981 and 1983. They seek a declaratory judgment to the effect that the rules, regulations and procedures of the Board are unconstitutional because they require, permit or sanction racially segregated public schools.

As I had learned intuitively, at Manhasset High, there was what educators came to call a wide "achievement gap," which, prior to decisions like **Blocker versus Board,** was attributed not to educational segregation but to differences in IQ and learning ability between the black and white populations.

Right away, upon seeing this case in the law book, I knew Ralph had won it, because not long after I graduated ol' MHS, the Valley School along with the Plandome Road School up on the hill, were both razed and replaced with Manhasset's first integrated, elementary school, the Shelter Rock Road School. Both populations were bussed in. It had taken me twenty years to learn, but I at last started to understood how heroic Ralph Blocker really was.

The court's heart must surely have been in the right place, as the discrimination in my hometown was rampant, and not only towards blacks. However, the court's decision may or may not have helped the situation as, unwittingly, this and cases like it led to a movement towards *school consolidation.* Consolidation and the comprehensive school movement would usher in 40 years of bussing kids into larger and larger high schools, schools of a size that turned out to be lower performing, less safe, and riddled with hidden costs.

For many students, our large, consolidated schools became and remain forbidding places where cliques of students roam about segregating themselves even further. Had educators or educational psychologists and not lawyers divided up the schools, they might have integrated them but left them the same, small size. 160, the size of the Valley School, would have been a great size for integrating and connecting across groups, and for teachers developing emotionally significant relationships with diverse kids.

We now know that large schools promote the separateness they were set up to prevent. Our larger schools produce more crime and vandalism, lower achievement, more cliques, higher drop-out rates, and more teacher drop-outs. We now know that small schools promote egalitarianism, flexibility, and inclusiveness. Fifty years have gone by. Could it be that the United States government, however well intentioned, has spent trillions of dollars over the past 50 years to create large, comprehensive schools which were intended to integrate kids despite unclear and conflicting evidence showing how integration could or has occurred in them? The Public Policy Institute of California's extensive, longitudinal research resulted in bigger questions than answers, such as: "Turning to the analysis of test scores, what do the generally insignificant effects of [school] choice on achievement imply for state and national policy?"

When will we look at successful integration models? Such questions, almost too big to ask, suggest the rarely acknowledged reality: we continue to put kids into large, hierarchical school communities focused on imposed and enforced rules and unequal divisions of labor and, for no reason supported by any evidence, we suppose the outcomes will be fairness, democratic decision-making, cohesiveness and cooperation.

Widely held myths governed educational thinking when I was a kid. One was that intelligence and learning style were set, so that there was little point providing integrated classes—in this way we pretended there was nothing political at all about providing minorities with underfunded schools.

Later on, another myth came along that, if you only create bigger, more comprehensive school organizations, kids would mix more and seize more opportunities. That myth hasn't panned out at all, either. In schools, governments and corporations, the past few generations of larger and larger institutions that were supposed to make things more efficient have only made life more complicated, disconnected, and unmanageable. Needless to say, as bad as it was in the Valley School for kids like Ralph and Jimmy, the data shows that gangs, crime, and racial strife have only gotten worse in our schools nationwide. Our comprehensive schools are too big to be safe and inclusive.

Maybe Ralph should have let Jimmy just drop me, as though some natural law were playing out, and then the whole future might have played out differently—maybe then we could have had an honest look at how suspended in space we all are, so that schools could have held supportive relationships as a core value rather than bigness. We're all hanging on to one another, but we rarely see it. The world is a dangerous place and it is trust we need to be building, not gigantic social systems that need perpetual legal and legislative maintenance.

Smaller schools produce higher academic performance and a greater sense of connection between and among groups, even diverse ones. Generations before *Blocker versus Board*, we found out that the American Indian groups would do anything, including die, to resist being removed from their families and communities and becoming "re-educated" as Americans. Without question, the original Manhasset and other Long Island Indian tribes got off even worse than any of us, and they disappeared from the earth with barely a trace along with their language, Algonquin.

Our failed social engineering to indoctrinate Indian kids was evident to everyone, as though our government at last heard The Great Law of the Iroquois Confederacy: "In our every deliberation, we must consider the impact of our decisions on the next seven generations." Of course, the United States eventually allowed the re-opening of locally-based, tribal schools, and our Indian tribes are still in recovery. But desegregating our schools through the creation of institutions too big to govern will bring us nothing in seven generations. It's been fifty years already, and all the comprehensive schools in the world have never produced a lacrosse player better than Jimmy Brown.

"We find ourselves embedded in cultures that are, in many ways, mismatched with our neuroanatomy, neurobiology, and basic social instincts," Cozolino writes. "The most successful institutions are able to integrate the instinctual imperatives of our trial brains into the structures of contemporary hierarchical organizations." 200 or 250 are just about the perfect cap on size for a connected and safe school organization, as well as for our post-tribal minds and their needs for a bit more complexity. About the only thing you should surely predict to produce when you make a school larger than 250 and especially when it gets larger than 400 is a steroidal lacrosse team. But then, American Indian settlements were often less than 200, and they invented lacrosse. Games for tribes larger than that had a different name: war.

*What if schools held supportive relationships
as a core value rather than bigness?*

Photo by Johnny King, The Grauer School.

"We learn better when we are face-to-face and heart-to-heart with someone who cares about us."

—Louis Cozolino

Bigness
(We've Got to Fight, Boys)

To what extent do we all presume the stature of "bigness" in America?

According to my niece Danielle, when she was in her sophomore year of college, she asked the professor in the very first class of her first-ever college math course a question about the law of cosines. The professor responded that she should major in math, so she did. Applied Mathematical Sciences.

Now, we are en route from Austin to College Park for her graduation from Texas A&M University. We approach the campus but the roads are windy and we keep getting lost. This is a maze. Eventually we find Danielle on the corner; there she is, texting at the coffee shop. We drive towards the George Bush Presidential Library, on campus and not far from the Intramural Fields, taking wrong turns the whole way. I blame the new iPhone mapping app. Although it is commonplace to be lost on this campus of 48,000 students, almost everyone seems understanding of that and smiles at you saying, "Howdy." That's the Aggie way. That's one of the main things that drew Danielle to A&M. Plus, there are 800 clubs you can join. Danielle said she had friends who were from farm towns with populations smaller than the lecture classes they attended.

The Commencement Convocation was to be held that evening and the actual commencement the next day. I did not want to miss either. Since I run a high school graduation every year, and have for many years, I've become a graduation fan. I seek out graduations every chance I get. I take notes at them. I hope I'm not just compensating for my own lackluster high school graduation, which I don't remember at all. Through the years, I have methodically enriched and refined my own commencement exercises with program notes from the best of them: Harvard Law School, University of San Diego, Sarah Lawrence College, The Bishop's School of La Jolla, independent international schools in Europe, and even elementary school graduations. I once even attended a graduation for dogs—I'm like a graduation hound. Personally, I find The Grauer School graduation to be the most beautiful and moving of them all.

It is Convocation time (called elsewhere the baccalaureate). Once the luminaries are all assembled on the stage, we rise for Invocation recited by the student body president, who is to graduate the next day. Then, "Howdy," the university president says. There are 360,000 living alumni of Texas A&M, he points out, so the new grads will have them as extended family all around the world and at job interviews.

An advisor to some U.S. presidents is introduced next. "Howdy," she begins. "I commend you through the eyes of my own parents." Nice line. She asks the graduates to give their parents a hand. Great gesture, I think, and make a note to do this the next time I preside at graduation. "You are twenty-first century champions of freedom," she follows. I don't think I'll use that one. Then she tells stories about "Pappy Bush," whom she admires deeply. Good material. The elder Bush president is in the hospital at the moment and no one really knows what will happen.

After some time, the university president takes the stage again and closes the Convocation ceremonies saying, "We want you to continue your engagement with Texas A&M." The school anthem, a football fighting song, comes on: "The Spirit of Aggieland." ("For we are the Aggies—the Aggies so true...")

Then we go out for a family Tex-Mex dinner.

Next day, we make our way to the diploma ceremony. Despite the masses, we're swept right in with hardly a line. The end of the basketball arena is staged with the largest drapery we've ever seen; a curtain at least 50 feet high. From up above, we look out and down across a sea of floating mortarboards which some of the graduation candidates have decorated, perhaps so parents and friends can try to find them. But for us, the crowd is so thick we are starting to realize there's a fair chance we will not be able to see my niece at all. Just then, the mom behind us spies her child and sends a shriek out across the stadium in the hope that her daughter will know she's been identified. Will this daughter recognize mom's shriek?

We receive a text message. "I am next to the girl with the gold flower glued on her cap." But as the procession nears an end, seats completely filling the basketball court, we still cannot find Danielle or the gold flower.

Now the president is taking the podium as Danielle's boyfriend's father takes his seat beside us after a 14-hour drive from Nebraska.

"Howdy," the president intones. "We're celebrating yer' success today. Altogether, we're graduating 3,375 of you today and tomorrow." We trust Danielle is in there. We try texting back, but no luck. Danielle had informed us just that morning that there'd been some trouble with the computerized transcript program. Our school back home graduates around twenty-five students a year, introducing and telling stories about each one personally, but even we have computer troubles like this. The boyfriend's father goes off with his camera to try to find Danielle and take a photograph.

A member of the Board of Regents ascends to the podium for the "Authorization to Confer Degrees." At a graduation, it's helpful if someone stands up and provides verification that the diploma is backed by some legitimate authority. I don't recall seeing it done this way before, and make careful notes. I wonder, are we authorizing our diplomas well enough back home?

"Howdy," he says. "Many of you will be leaving Aggieland to pursue your dreams . . ." the ceremony continues . . . "Congratulations and beat the hell out of Oklahoma," he implores, conveying full confidence in the stature such a beating would bear on the Aggie sheepskin, at least in this part of the world.

Next up is the "Induction into The Association of Former Students." We know what this means. "Will the degree candidates please rise?" It means that alumni donation appeal letters are already in the mail. "By virtue of the authority vested in me by the Charter of the Association of Former Students ..." I was scribbling fast now—I want such a charter at my school.

We get a text message! Danielle is in section 120 or 121.

". . . giving back to the school as alumni . . ." the Charter continues. That's code for, "Donate to the annual fund every year." We're scouring the mortarboards again.

Now the president is returning to the center stage, asking "Will the graduates rise . . ." He is preparing to shake 2000 hands. He discourages "bone crushing grips" and encourages any reasonable alternatives to shaking, so as to save his hand. Fist bumps. Hugs. Be creative.

The various deans begin calling the names of the graduates. "Candidates for Commissions in the Armed Forces of the United States: Tyler John Baldauf . . ."

"Doctor of Education: Amber Lea Dankert." Both northern (Amber) and southern (Dankert) European heritages, a blend, I think, as the names start to spool. In America, even here in Texas, those distinctions have blurred.

Danielle's mother Flo, who has not yet found her daughter, and who was up half the night with the computerized transcript problem, points out that we might be able to see

Danielle on the black jumbotron TV scoreboards suspended from the ceiling.

"Doctor of Philosophy: Chun-Chu Chen."

We're settled into a comfortable flow. The President has figured out that there will be three seconds per student. (At Pepperdine Law Commencement in Malibu it was seven seconds per grad, nine seconds at Bates College in Maine.) It's going to be two hours no matter what. I'd flown 2,000 miles for those three seconds. We scan a bit more for Danielle. But we've adjusted to the scale of this whole show, and we know she'll come around in good time. I have a little emailing on my smartphone to catch up on anyway; I understand that I'm complicit in modern disruptive technology.

Now we've gone through Masters of Real Estate, Agribusiness, and are up to Bachelors of Spacial Science, then Rangeland Ecology and Management.

"Is that her? Look, is that Danielle?" Flo asks.

No, it's not her, but Flo figures out that Danielle would have to be in the second to last row on the far side. We've been looking completely in the wrong section.

The College of Science Dean is up now. "Biology: Francisco Adolfo Barrios . . . Bret Shannon Taylor." Hispanic and Irish, I figure. The names are amazing. The students all have three names, and most of them express two or even three different nationalities for their roots. I give the whole idea of ethnicity in American maybe three more generations of relevance. The president shows no sign of wear as the two people assigned to hand diplomas to him keep them flowing. They can't hand out a single wrong one! But they seem confident. After all, these are folks who manage a football arena that holds 40,000. That's about the size of a typical Roman Empire city. Their quarterback has just won the Heisman trophy.

And at last we reach page 29 of the program, Danielle's page. Our hearts quicken.

Danielle's group has risen, we're sure of it, and have proceeded down the side aisle, taking their places in line leading up to the podium. "Applied Mathematical Sciences." Yes! We look madly for her, scanning the line from front to back, but she is not in there. She must be in there ... but what of the computer transcript thing? We go down to the railings and lean over but none of us can find her anywhere.

"Danielle Andrea Grauer," we hear over a long-range acoustical sound throw, oh my God. There! That is actually her ascending the portable steps unit to the stage. Now she is hugging the president just as she had planned in advance, to save his hand, as we fumble for our cameras, but it is too late for that. Now she is walking off the other side of the stage and we are clapping and maybe screaming a little. I have a grainy photo of the back of her head, with her waving somewhere, just after the hug.

Soon, the last student walks, and then, "You are graduating today from a very unique, American institution . . ." the president is saying. And continuing, " . . . [something] using the Aggie spirit . . . [something] . . . may turn your Aggie ring..."

> But our minds are elsewhere.
> Now the anthem is resounding and people are everywhere...
> *We are the Aggies—the Aggies we are,*
> *True to each other as Aggies can be.*
> *We've got to fight, boys,*
> *We've got to fight!*

Once in our car, we are ushered out of the parking lot, right through a sort of toll where you get a tee shirt if you sign up for the alumni association. Then we go out for Hunan and Cantonese food.

*Paopao School in French Polynesia gets the same
curriculum as schools in Paris, France.*

"Everybody is a genius. But if you judge a fish by its ability to climb a tree, it will live its whole life believing that it is stupid."
—Albert Einstein

The Black Horse of Tahiti

Are the measurable goals in student achievement more valuable than the immeasurable ones? To what extent do we expect teachers to pass along our culture?

Patrick Bourlegeaux is one of the best surfers I know, hitting lips and getting warm-water barrels from his home base in French Polynesia. By day, Patrick misses many of the best waves in his role as principal of the Paopao School on the tropical island of Moorea.

After a magic, early morning surf session at a perfect reef pass I am not at liberty to name, we pulled a palm frond-wrapped breadfruit we had picked from the hillside behind Patrick's house out of the coals and sliced it up for breakfast. A neighbor wandered by with some lobster he just pulled out of the water—it was Patrick's friend, Arsene Harehoe, the legendary surfer, the one they call The Black Horse. Arsene has dark eyes and the somber affect of a heavy surf rider, as though he has encountered forces of nature that would silence most people. As though the things that happen on land are the small things. Or maybe it is the French influence.

Filled up, we parted from Arsene and a few other surfers who had gathered around, and we drove up the coconut palm-fringed coastline past a house on stilts, a fisherman's beached handmade outrigger canoe nestled under the shade of a banyan tree, a stand with fresh-caught, shiny yellow and green dorado fish hanging and ready to be sliced up into sushi; a large, wooden fishing boat broken to pieces on shore from a day that must have been terrible and heavy, and, then heading north, we passed a couple high-end, international resorts which provide tourists with a friendly caricature of the tropical island life. Things looked idyllic on that day, but one can still see that the locals live with elements that can be unforgiving. Soon we pulled into the Paopao school, with it's green roofs blending into the surrounding jungle that rose abruptly. Giant cumulous clouds backed up into the sharp, mossy green mountains, cloistering the little school like a lost world.

This is Patrick's other life and, as he graciously allowed me to take over some classes, I was at first surprised by something. The curriculum is controlled tightly by the French government. In other words, the teachers in French Polynesia are expected to teach the same exact things as the teachers in the citadel brick schools of Paris.

How can this be? Will they study the Reo Mā`ohi language and the spirit it conveys? Millennia ago, their Polynesian forefathers, in brave journeys across vast oceans, navigated water currents, wind and stars of great complexity to conjure and track destinations so that they could continue to live. Does it matter? The students have a completely different heritage than Parisian kids. How can Patrick even allow this loss of a world? Is he really just a government bureaucrat? A colonialist?

But, then, how can he allow me to teach in such an institution?

"How can kids from both cultures possibly need the same schooling?" I ask Patrick.

He casts his eyes down and looks resigned, bored even. There is no point in confronting a history of such great confusion and loss. "It is all too much. There is nothing I can do," he replies. I do not believe him.

Afterwards we went back to Patrick's office and had mugs

of coffee with Eagle Brand, and I felt like we had been out at sea. He gathered folders and documents for me while I sat on a flat sofa with aluminum arm rails and sipped the lukewarm, sugary drink. Then he handed me the papers, a crisp stack of French curricular documents from the French Department of Education, National Core Study, "to assist Core French teachers at the Grade K-6 levels by providing the parameters for the delivery of the program." It detailed the philosophy, content, objectives, methodology and evaluation associated with the various standard dimensions of the curriculum, and it was the last thing I wanted to carry with me around French Polynesia. I had no idea why he was giving it to me, except I was worried he thought it was his duty.

I scanned the opening page which said "As we move rapidly towards the 21st century, its challenge is to offer students a school experience that reflects a contemporary . . . *something, something* . . . skills and attitudes that are of most worth to the individual and to society," searched Patrick's unknowable, European face, and packed the documents away. The year was 2012.

There was still time before lunch, and Patrick signaled me, expeditiously: "Come with me," and we boarded his van, silently rounded a few bends in the road until we reached a sandy beachfront sheltered darkly with dense palms and a shack where small, fiberglass catamarans were lined up on racks and on the sand. Outside, in the calm, turquoise bay, the little ones, Patrick's students, were learning the art of sailing, right in the middle of the school day, and Patrick looked nothing like he did back in the school office. Now his eyes gleamed as he pointed to one after another little sailor managing the bright yellow and orange sails, all future watermen. He waved. From the boats, the little ones waved back in delight. Inside, several little ones were puzzling over block and tackle set-ups and sorting out lines.

"Doesn't all this sailing cut directly into the time these kids are supposed to be studying the state curriculum," I asked? "Won't this affect their test scores? Are you in breach of French law, risking your job here?"

"Yes," Patrick said. "I think there is really no time for this at all. Especially if you follow the required schedule, but this does not matter. Because I also think the sailing will raise their scores."

It was one of those statements that is really more of a question to ponder than it is a fact to believe. But I believed it anyway, completely. It is much truer than the kind of truth you can prove. "And, you know," he added, "if we would measure their joy, it would raise those scores, too." I had more questions, but just then Patrick saw a student on the shoreline heading for a landing and he moved quickly over to the water's edge to help. This one could be the next Black Horse one day and he would need to be strong and skilled against the elements and hospitable in the ways of Polynesia.

Zuni girl in traditional dance garb.

"You may house their bodies but not their souls,
For their souls dwell in the house of tomorrow, which you cannot
visit, not even in your dreams.
You may strive to be like them, but seek not to make them like
you.
For life goes not backward nor tarries with yesterday."
—Khalil Gibran

Indians of Six Nations

Are basic survival skills and living off the land worth teaching about? Who will teach them?

Once we recommit to pursuing our genuine curiosity we can start to reclaim our intuitions. That way, answers can come to us in the most natural way in the world, and the world becomes our teacher again. With this intention in mind, I love this story.

William and Mary College in Williamsburg, Virginia, is the second oldest college in the United States. It was founded in 1693 through a charter and funds granted by King William III and Queen Mary II. Many famous Americans are among the former students, including U.S. Presidents Thomas Jefferson, James Monroe, and John Tyler. Also, George Washington received his surveyor's license from William and Mary in 1749 and later served as chancellor of the college.

As excerpted from *Letters of a Nation* by A. Carroll, in 1744, the College of William and Mary invited the Indians of the Six Nations (now known as the Iroquois) to send twelve young men to be "properly" educated. Soon after, William and Mary received the following reply from the Six Nations:

Sirs,

We know that you highly esteem the kind of learning taught in Colleges, and that the Maintenance of our young Men, while with you, would be very expensive to you. We are convinc'd, therefore, that you mean to do us Good by your Proposal; and we thank you heartily. But you, who are wise, must know that different Nations have different Conceptions of things; and you will therefore not take it amiss, if our Ideas of this kind of Education happen not to be the same with yours. We have had some Experience of it. Several of our Young People were formerly brought up at the Colleges of the Northern Provinces; they were instructed in all your Sciences; but, when they came back to us, they were bad Runners, ignorant of every means of living in the Woods, unable to take a Deer, or kill an Enemy, spoke our Language imperfectly, were neither fit for Hunters, Warriors, nor Counsellors; they were totally good for nothing. We are, however not the less oblig'd by your kind Offer, tho' we decline accepting it; and, to show our grateful Sense of it, if the Gentlemen of Virginia will send us a Dozen of their Sons, we will take care of their Education, instruct them in all we know, and make Men of them.

Finding toads in California Central Valley.

"Come away, O human child!
To the waters and the wild
With a faery, hand in hand,
For the world's more full of weeping than you can understand."
—W.B. Yeats

"I could draw its map by heart,
showing its contours,
strata and vegetation
name every height,
small burn and lonely sheiling ..."

—WH Auden

The Moon in a Jar

What unconscious beliefs from our own early lives now guide the behaviors, emotions, and thoughts we have as educators? How can we be better listeners?

Behind my childhood home in Manhasset, Long Island, were thick woods. My earliest memories are of running wild through the narrow, leaf-covered paths on summer nights. I remember filling my pockets with eye-catching stones—some for gathering and arranging, some for throwing and hunting. I've read that fireflies are hard to find these days, but they weren't back then. On summer nights, we illuminated glass jars with fireflies we had caught from around the low hanging tree branches—a moon of my own in a jar—then set them free the next day. Back then, we were free to roam, to take, to give and to run as far as our legs would take us.

On my sixth birthday, we all sensed something in the works, as land movers made their first clearance into my childscape. "Maybe they are putting in a park," I remember saying to my dad with visions of greenery. He didn't know. I was too young to experience hate, and I hope I always will be, but on my seventh birthday, I strapped on my gun belt, unholstered my six-shooters and, peering through the chain linked fence that now stood where I once ran and climbed trees, I snapped off rounds of caps towards "The Miracle Mile" with its B. Altmans, JJ Newberry's 5 & 10, and Davega's jumbo sporting goods and appliance store.

I became masterful at hopping that fence, even though the chain links were topped with barbs. Eventually, with a hacksaw, I simply cut out an opening so that it formed a "V" and we could just slip right through like passing into twilight. I zigzagged through the cars spread across the vast, black, macadam lot where, for centuries beforehand, rabbits, robins and spiders had coexisted in their natural habitat, now gone forever. I could disappear for mornings or afternoons into the alleys and doorways of the shops and enter into the new, florescent-lit micro-climate with no sense of the forest expiry, too young to weep for the weight of history, the loss of our woods and fertile brown soil, the death of a squirrel beneath a skip loader.

There in the mall, in our packs of two or three kids, we roamed, weaving in and out of stores, learning the best aisles and stairways as if they were hidden passages to elves' grottos or caves. It wasn't like roaming in the wooded wilds. But it was a new kind of wild, and our instinct to play was unabated as we looked subconsciously for new "species." We collected all that was alluring, lining our pockets with trinkets. One day a 5-cent candy bar. Another day a pencil charm. A pack of Juicy Fruit gum. Gathering in the wild became the game and we became unwitting, masterful, light-fingered thieves. "Let's go on a hocking spree," one of my brothers suggested one day. And from then on our activity was branded innocent and subversive at once, a paradox accessible only to children. We slipped though the chain link passage into a netherworld of linoleum aisles where we roamed and chased and escaped.

Miracles! Stalking a Rawlings genuine leather hardball in Davega's—aromatic and sensual—stuffing it into our clothing, then making our cunning getaway, endorphins rushing hard. Only humans can lie, and only a human child can lie purely. Like many others who lose their lands, we had become poachers and smugglers. For me, this all occurred in a sort of dreamstate. I don't recall having much guilt about any of it until at around age 10, my mother asked, "You don't have any money—where did you get that baseball scorebook?" And at that point the truth sunk in and what had seemed like an essential dream ended for me. No longer was I a fearless adventurer, nor was I, in the truest sense, a child.

I forgot about this shame for at least 40 years and all the while childhood changed. Over this time, we watched the walk to school disappear. Slashed to the minimum were the lunch hours and aimless breaks. Gone was the free play along with over half of the world's forests. Gone were the games with no rules or boundaries. Though I had held on to my youth in many unpredictable ways, throughout a teaching career I attempted, with varying measures of success, to conform to the weatherless world of desks in rows and time periods that ended with drilling buzzers that apportioned out four minutes of relative freedom. But all the while, somehow, nature stayed a part of me. It snowed inside of me, dropped leaves in me, washed upon my shores and then, one evening, surveying the raw, future site of The Grauer School, a sense of loss and longing possessed my spirit again. We stood at the highest place on the lot and contemplated what we might do with five acres of coastal sage and maritime chaparral, and I at last could see what was meant by the terribly good lessons from my dark past. The shopping mall, "The Miracle Mile," had separated me from my natural world, attempted to exile me from my childhood. But I had never fully let go and now, restitution.

We built our school and left behind a two-acre, sloped corridor for native habitat and wildlife. It includes sage, wild radish, pepper grass, wild cucumber, morning glory and honeysuckle. Making their living off of these commons are lizards, hummingbirds, owls, wrens, endangered gnatcatchers, four different kinds of sparrows and more birds, squirrels and woodrats and snakes, and 24 kinds of butterflies. Restoring and maintaining this hillside to pristine condition became a part of our development plan. And so, we preserved our wilds and shall forever be short of parking.

This corridor of nature is home to science teachers, teens dreaming of a first kiss and students looking for a quiet wander. Artists sketch here. Student poets write verses beneath the Mexican elderberry here. I hope history students will come here, too. Perhaps they will see the timeline from here all the way back to the Act of Enclosure of Victorian England, the cruel act by which the vulnerable commoners were fenced out for the entitlement of the privileged few, essentially exiling the country folk from the land. In her gorgeous book entitled *Kith*, Welsh author Jay Griffiths writes of those enclosures as extended metaphors for so much of the sadness in schools today. She writes, "This is part of the answer to the riddle of childhood unhappiness: their minds need, and deserve, a whole world of utterly unfenceable freedom where everything has othering, everything is radiant with the possibilities of elseness."

Today's exiles are our kids in rows of chairs, in fenced-in "consolidated" schools, left on weekends to roam the digital media one step ahead of their parents, or to join field games where adults make all the rules and where their lives are hardly grounded to real earth for days on end. How can they even know what wilds once lay on the other side, before the fence was there? What could possibly be more valuable than the wilds or the freedom there? How can we teach our children about all that?

Maasai Elder at Emboreet School.

"This is the setting out.
The leaving of everything behind.
Leaving the social milieu. The preconceptions.
The definitions. The language. The narrowed field
of vision. The expectations.
No longer expecting relationships, memories, words, or letters to
mean what they used to mean. To be, in a word: Open."
—Rabbi Lawrence Kushner

A Refugee

What keeps us in this work?

The new kid came in his first morning saying he'd dreamt of a ghost in the school. "There's a ghost in this school," he muttered, eyes cast down with a vulnerable smile. He had just come down from NorCal. No jobs up there. No water. Soil of lost virtue.

No jobs, just the faded apparition of green hills filled with life and promise, turned to long landscapes of hazy brown, rolling hills stretching out under an indigo sky, the thin farm settlements scattered like Bedouin encampments. Families reduced to drinking water from a spoon up there, the farmers liked to say, blaming the politicians for the climate. It was English class. We were going to read Poe that day, maybe. "Did you bring 'em down from San Luis Reservoir," I asked him. "The ghosts."

"Crow's Landing," he said with half his voice. He sat a little slope-shouldered, what you might call a bit scrawny, oily face and hair. Probably been pushed around some by mean kids.

"Who cares," spoke the other kids' body language through subtle patterns in their rows.

"What are you really looking for?" I asked them all, though I should have been teaching Poe.

I was five years in. The presence of nervous parents and the testing norms of other schools and somehow just the general sense of society's worn-out conception of schooling was like a press, like a suffocation. If I wasn't going to be one of those educators shuttling through it all, through the grey, shuttling towards the pension, and I wasn't going to be one of those alternative activists who attack the system no matter what and teach class out of that Howard Zinn book, what was I going to be? It would have been good to be in this class, wrapped in a discussion, bringing the new farm kid in. I was trying to learn to ask questions that evoke silence before speech, and to seek out the silence as though it were a cold wind that my students should bear into.

I just wanted to talk real and not fear silence. But of course, not everyone wants to listen to a cold wind, and especially not kids in Southern California, in English class. I was losing track of why we were all there together, in this class.

It was almost unknowable that the real reason Gus was here was simply that there was still water piping in down here as opposed to up there in Crow's Landing. Crow's Landing, where the farmland was faltering, civilization's silent broken record.

He was living with his grandmother now, a kind soul with a perpetually sad look on her face, who had owned a beach house down here since the 70s when they were quite cheap to buy, when people still thought it was too foggy along the coast. She took him in, her daughter's boy, like she would also donate a kidney to her . . . even if her daughter was to blame for her own kidney failure from hard living. It would take us another year to learn that she had lied on Gus's application. Like half his classmates up there, he'd been suspended from the local school, and the other half were leaving town. His parents were in the middle of losing their home, and when their oldest daughter committed suicide, they gave up waiting for another dam project and divorced. All this would come out later, and then Gus would get his scholarship yanked and have to go to public school, where he would grow into his fists and his loneliness and loss would look like anger. His grandmother's voice would grow thin and dry as she tried to get him to talk at dinnertimes.

"Tell me about the ghost," I said.

It was good to have someone bring something new into our system, something to challenge the stasis. I was already beginning to grow weary of students pretending to fit in. I longed for some vague sense of connection across barriers that people fear or have no regard for and much of my short teaching career had already been dedicated to seeking that out, sometimes only to end up feeling like a refugee from a Paul Bowles story. In fact, I had traveled substantially. And now, here was everything right in my class.

Gus had been sent down from the barren lands of water wars to one of the very beach towns that was now receiving the water his parents would have used for crops had they prevailed over the politicians. But they had not. Now we could buy produce grown in Mexico, cheap, and so the water was more valuable to us for making our lawns green instead or showering out our hair conditioner in warm pulsations.

Gus sat shotgun by my teacher's desk and didn't answer. The students in the back rows slumped, and it would take about a year for Gus to be back there, too, and after that he'd be gone. Later that day, I watched them all out on the green, moving in patterns before drifting back into their other classes. Then I sat down at my desk and graded their homework papers. I was wishing there was something I could do to know students faster and better, and years later I would. Eventually, after traveling enough miles, I would give up knowing what to presume about almost anybody, which made some things like encouragement and trust easier, and I grew happy I'd stayed in this work, this profession.

Author sharing text messages with Maasai guide in Africa.

"They are small things. They don't end poverty, they don't lift us from underdevelopment, they don't socialize the means of production nor of exchange, they won't expropriate the caves of Ali Baba. But, perhaps, they unchain the joy of doing, and translate into actions. Because after all, taking action in the real world and changing it, despite the little that change may be, is the only way to prove that reality is transformable."
—Eduardo Galeano

Afterword
About These Stories / *An Origin Tale*

The Stories of *Fearless Teachers* were prompted by some assumptions about the difficult state of our field and why so many people are leaving it. These assumptions are illustrated in the following story:

An Origin Tale

Once upon a time there was a nation whose schools grew larger and larger—for well over a hundred years, there was continuous expansion. Districts grew as they added layers of workers and a great many consultants to manage technology and standards, and even more layers to control and manage the added ones. School reform focused primarily on "accountability" measures — or, how to hold students, teachers, principals, schools and districts accountable for higher standardized-test scores, but, these reforms did not address most of the real problems children faced in their classrooms and daily lives.

Class size grew. Management grew. And so, educators grew further removed from real, live kids. Schools and districts grew so large and complex that, at last, on average, half of their workers rarely even talked with students or looked into their eyes. Even the organizations that studied and evaluated these big organizations were growing. Corporations spawned to manage ever bigger government contracts, and agencies spawned to regulate those. American students spent billions of hours a year being bussed in to consolidated schools where growing numbers of them would write essays that could be graded by computers, and then disappear. Even more troubling, every single day, thousands of students would drop out, disconnected, with almost none of their talents ever standing a chance of reaching the classrooms of a university. Who could explain this?

Increasingly, good teachers were leaving the profession, even while some good ones stayed on. Researchers continued surveying the dissolving local systems as though they were watching foreign habitat loss, all the while documenting while nodding their heads back and forth. Some of the biggest states were experiencing alarming drops in teacher training enrollment. The role of teacher was disassociating from the classical definition of mentor and scholar and a headline in the nation's largest teaching journal read: "Anyone Can Be A Teacher."

The human child's desire for freedom is unquenchable, but there was diminishing time and space in school life to express their freedom. So, naturally, some families and teachers began looking for alternatives. For instance, hundreds of classes were offered on electronic, digital screens with the promise of customization, but that led to the erosion of thousands of hours of eye-to-eye human contact and millions of personal conversations. Where were the warm-blooded people? Where were the stories amidst the sea of big data and controlled systems? Where were the schools that enabled students and teachers to love school again? The seekers of options both in and out of traditional settings began searching the world and at first were discouraged by what they found. The very word "alternative" was seen as a weakness, connoting marginal, or threatening by most people in the field of education. In one community school, 100% of the students and teachers claimed they liked school, but since the school was small people just assumed *the data was invalid or that the school was not for normal kids. As they searched father afield, it turned out that bigness as a disease in schools was not a problem polarized only to America.*

Teachers and families all over the world were lost or losing hope, and many were angry. Without a hint of irony, the most entrenched corporate, government, and institutional players involved in education routinely referred to themselves as "reformers." What's more, the "reforms" normally had little to do with the dreams and aspirations of teachers and students. And the disillusioned teachers and families kept looking for something else. They didn't care if the schools were public or private.

They just kept looking. In time, they began finding more educational oases that fell outside the trends, apart from all the bureaucracy, corporatization, and bigness. With enough excavation, they found pockets of democracy and laughter, where people seemed not to care at all about hundred-year trends in school and district up-sizing. They found extraordinary, un-replicable, off-the-radar stories of teachers and students who never turned up in the data crunches of research universities or think tank experiments launched by dot.com billionaires and global publishing corporations. They found pockets of democracy where people reclaimed the meaning of the title, teacher. And in these pockets, the seekers of new, alternative educational methodologies began to notice a simple thing: whenever authentic human relationships could somehow reclaim their place over systems and controls, the people in schools were feeling safer and happier again.

Continuing the search, they found places where the schools reflected a genuine expression of their communities rather than of the larger governments serving to homogenize them. In these places, they found story—messy, unpredictable, struggling human story. They found possibility in the far off mountains, in little and long given up on logging towns, among courageous girl groups willing to risk their lives, and some even rediscovered possibility in their own minds. They found inspired teaching in under-the-

radar classrooms in schools that were labeled hopeless. They found it both on and off the grid and through unexpected portals. They even found possibility in hopelessness! Fearless teachers risked their jobs, and some lost them. Nevertheless, as more and more teachers chose human connection over and above bureaucracy, big systems and regulation, people began loving their schools again. Are people like that small and alone, or is there something we can learn from them and pass along?

*****

In these stories, passionate, observant teachers and students are often found doing what they are not expected to do, all in an expression of personal freedom and a yearning for a unified and authentic human connection. These are stories of people quietly reclaiming our profession.

A chapter and core metaphor for this book, "The Moon in a Jar," reflects a trade-off, and was the working title for the book for many months: Can we take a natural force, like the moon and, by capturing it, control it? As *Education Week* noted in 2015, "None of the predominantly psychological barriers identified by researchers is going to be overcome by more technology, more data, more tests, or a plan to crush teachers' unions" (Walters, p. 25).

As I was writing, books and videos on reliable teaching methods were proliferating—this is of course not one of them—but, as stories such as "The Gaokao Cowboy" illustrate, those are usually manuals for control of human behavior, rather than supportive in the areas of student empowerment, connection, creativity and authentic discovery. Despite efforts towards standardization, school cultures include unique histories and aspirations, and casts of irrepressible heroes and villains, and these are what make them worth going to. The free expression of this diverse cast of characters teaching children are what can keep our field alive and resonant and keep us in the field. Sadly, many students and teachers were losing the will to show up.

One story, "What the Revolution Looked Like," documents an event that occurred early in the career of my friend and old college roommate, Tony, as he learned the hard way that, if you seriously listen to your students, your lesson plans might not pan out as expected. Tony became superintendent of schools in a large, affluent, and high performing New York suburban district, and he wrote to me, very privately, "Here in [. . .] we still hold to certain principles in spite of the Common Core and other red-tape garbage."

So it had come to this. Despite our best efforts to create nationally controlled curricula with a reliable if not automated delivery system, whether it be in other nations around the world or the United States, I was learning everywhere I traveled that, as often as not, the main point of teaching was to avoid all this.

"Inside the classroom, with a teacher who cares and wants only the best for his kids, it can happen anywhere," Tony wrote, though his school board must never hear him. Here Tony was describing the foot soldiers of schooling who press on, undeterred by forces too complex and large to ever know. These are our silent heroes, really. Many of them think few radical thoughts beyond those that tempt their students, behind the classroom door. But maybe, as Tracy Chapman sang, "Talk about a revolution sounds like whispers." As I eventually grasped in the "Navajo School" chapter, "Time after time in my work as a teacher, I've witnessed the sheer delight students and teachers take in doing nothing more than circling around, eyes drawn together, and discovering one another." Could this be what the revolution looks like?

"First, do not prevent learning." (The Socratic Oath)

Bibliography

A Personal challenge: What if I committed to the Socratic Oath not only in the classroom, but as a way of humility in all my relationships?

Introduction
Lehonan, Tom (teacher) in discussion with the author, February 2014.

The Wounded Ones
Griffiths, Jay. "Kith." July 31, 2013. http://www.youtube.com/watch?v=nW6Ozjjp3Co,

The Gaokao Cowboy
Ang, Kristiano, and Yenni Kwok. "Elite Boarding Schools Spreading Through Asia." *The New York Times*. December 23, 2012. http://www.nytimes.com/2012/12/24/world/asia/elite-boarding-schools-spreading-through-asia.html

Ameson Educational and Cultural Exchange Foundation. "Chinese Students and Extra-curricular Activities: A Waste of Time?" *The Voice: The Ameson Education Newsletter*, 1, 4, 2012. http://www.communityworksinstitute.org/cwjonline/essays/a_essaystext/grauer_china.html

Apple in Education. "One School in China Takes an Innovative Approach to Education. 2013. http://www.apple.com/education/profiles/rdfz/

Bergreen, Laurence. *Marco Polo from Venice to Xanadu*. New York: Alfred A. Knopf, 2007.

Bradsher, Keith. "China Toughens Its Restrictions on Use of the Interne." *The New York Times*, December 28, 2012. http://www.nytimes.com/2012/12/29/world/asia/china-toughens-restrictions-on-internet-use.html

Confucius. *The Great Learning, The Doctrine of the Mean*. Beijing, China: Sinolingua, 1996.

Deng, Peng. *Private Education in Modern China*. Santa Barbara, CA: Praeger, 1997.

"Fifteen Facts about China's Grueling Entrance Exam." CollegeStats. August 14, 2012. Accessed August 6, 2015. http://collegestats. org/2012/08/15-facts-about-chinas-grueling-college-entrance-exam/

Grauer, Stuart. "The Gaokao Cowboy: How National Examinations Impact Student Development." *Community Works Journal.*

Levin, Dan. "A Chinese Education, For a Price." *The New York Times,* November 21, 2012. http://www.nytimes.com/2012/11/22/world/ asia/in-china-schools-a-culture-of-bribery-spreads.html

McMurtrie, Beth. "China Continues to Drive Foreign-Student Growth in the United States." *The Chronicle of Higher Education,* November 12, 2012. http://chronicle.com/article/China C o n t i n u e s - t o - Drive/135700/

Ministry of Education of the People's Republic of China. "Application for the Scholarship of Chinese Government." http://www.moe.edu. cn/publicfiles/business/htmlfiles/moe/s3917/201007/91577.html

Ministry of Education of the People's Republic of China. "International Cooperation and Exchanges."http://www.moe.edu.cn/publicfiles/ business/htmlfiles/moe/moe_2813/index.html

Spencer, Kyle. " For Asians, School Tests are Vital Steppingstones." *The New York Times,* October 26, 2012. http://www.nytimes. com/2012/10/27/education/a-grueling-admissions-test-highlights- a-racial-divide.html

Waley, Arthur. *The Book of Songs: The Ancient Chinese Classic of Poetry.* New York: Grove Press, 1987.

Watanabe, Teresa. "Record Number of School Districts in State Face Bankruptcy. *Los Angeles Times,* May 21, 2012. http://latimesblogs. latimes.com/lanow/2012/05/school-districts-bankruptcy.html

Wong, Edward. "Test That Can Determine the Course of Life in China Gets a Closer Examination." *The New York Times,* June 30, 2012. http://www.nytimes.com/2012/07/01/world/asia/burden-of- chinas-college-entrance-test-sets-off-wide-debate.html

Yang, Jeff. "Are Your Kids Smart Enough for China's Toughest Test? *The Wall Street Journal,* June 26, 2012. http://blogs.wsj.com/ speakeasy/2012/06/26/are-your-kids-smart-enough-for-chinas- toughest-test/?blog_id=120&post_id=70589

Han (Happiness as a Measurable Outcome)

Economist Intelligence Unit. "The Learning Curve." Pearson, 2012. http:// thelearningcurve.pearson.com/the-report

"Happy Planet Index." New Economics Foundation, 2013. www. happyplanetindex.org/data/

Salmon, Andrew. "New South Korean President Park Vows to Make People Happy." *South China Morning Post*, February 26, 2013. http://www.scmp.com/news/asia/article/1158579/new-south-korean-president-park-geun-hye-vows-make-people-happy

Seoul International Education Forum. "Han (Happiness as a Measurable Educational Outcome)." *Seoul Education Research and Information Institute*.136, 2013.

The Manhasset Indians (Lacrosse and the Real History of Comprensive Schools in America)

Betts, Julian R., Lorien A. Rice, Andrew C. Zau, Y. Emily Tang, and Cory R. Koedel. "Does School Choice Work? Effects on Student Integration and Achievement." Public Policy Institute of California, 2006. www.ppic.org/content/pubs/report/R_806JBR.pdf

BLOCKER V. BOARD OF EDUCATION OF MANHASSET, NEW YORK. 2015. Print.

Cozolino, Louis. *The Social Neuroscience of Education*, New York: W.W. Norton and Company, Inc., 2013.

Grauer, Stuart. "The Manhasset Indians: Lacrosse and the Real History of Comprehensive Schools in America." *Community Works Journal*. http://www.communityworksinstitute.org/cwjonline/essays/a_essaystext/grauer_lacrosse.html#sthash.3DHspTW0.dpuf

Grauer, Stuart. "Small Versus Large Schools: The Truth About Equity, Cost, and Diversity of Programming in Small and Large Schools" *Community Works Journal*. http://www.communityworksinstitute.org/cwjonline/essays/a_essaystext/grauer_smallsch1.html#sthash.lC1fvCqr.dpuf

Grauer, Stuart and Christina Ryan. "Small Schools: The Myths, Reality, and Potential of Small Schools." *Community Works Journal*. http://www.communityworksinstitute.org/cwjonline/essays/a_essaystext/grauer_smallschools2.html#sthash.AZyfm3Us.dpuf

Kirp, David L. "Making Schools Work." *The New York Times*, May 19, 2012. http://www.nytimes.com/2012/05/20/opinion/sunday/integration-worked-why-have-we-rejected-it.html

"What Does Research Say About School District Consolidation?" Education Northwest, July 2011. www.educationnorthwest.org/resource/what-does-research-say-about-school-district-consolidation

Afterword

Berliner, David C., and Gene V. Glass. "Trust But Verify." *Improving*

Schools: What Works? 72, no. 5 (2015): 10-14. http://www.ascd.org/publications/educational-leadership/feb15/vol72/num05/Trust,-But-Verify.aspx

Walters, Garrison. "Dump Management 'Science,' and Change Learning Attitudes" by *Education Week*, January 28, 2015. http://www.edweek.org/ew/articles/2015/01/28/change-education-attitudes-not-just-management.html

Wild Horse Sanctuary, South Dakota.

Follow-Up Questions for Socratic Seminars and Groups

1. Introduction: An Open Field of Questions
Can we restore story to a world obsessed with data?

2. Prologue: The Socratic Oath
What if teachers had their own Hippocratic Oath?

3. In Praise of Hooky
How can we teach freedom within the confines of the school and classroom? Is freedom ours to teach?

4. What the Revolution Looked Like
As teachers, do we sometimes become so preoccupied with our own agendas that we forget to ask our students for theirs? Are we so driven to deliver the requirements that we honestly feel we have no time to listen?

5. Kindness
Hundreds of research studies document how nearly half of all teens feel hopeless, depressed, or alone at some point during the school year. Are teachers, parents and policy makers responsible for this? What aspects of school and classroom organization cause isolation and cliques?

6. An Alpine Idyll
Beyond our lesson plan, without the curriculum and the room, are we still teachers? Does all our training leave us with something essential that defines us as "teacher?" Is there a place for wisdom in school, or for elders?

7. Begin and Begin Again
How real are the lines on your resume? How much of ourselves dare we reveal to our students? What does it mean to be a teacher?

8. Tikkun Olam (Healing a Fearful World)
The great martyrs and leaders through history—Socrates, Confucius, Jesus, Siddhartha Gautama, Mohammed—were all called "teacher." Who is called a teacher today?

9. The Triumph of the Revolution
Can we imagine students and teachers being free and untethered to digital technology? Is it worth imagining?

10. Five Karibuni Stories (School Hopping in Tanzania)
What forms of teaching, schooling and culture are going extinct?

11. Extinction
It has long been believed by many that the purpose of the teacher is to pass along culture and tradition. What can we do if we see customs and traditions about to die in our own community?

12. A School Where the Old Village Acacia Tree Once Was
Will the teacher advance the goals of the state or is the place-based, local heritage equally worthy?

13. Blessing the Goat
How much will we risk just to seize a "teachable moment" that life serves up?

14. How Do You Educate a Warrior? (Emboreet)

How do you educate a warrior? Are warrior qualities relevant to schooling?

15. Unschooling

Where do students learn more at school, in or out of class? Is the role of the teacher to liberate or control students?

16. A Gateway

What does it feel like when you enter a campus? Does it feel safe? Do you feel connected or isolated in this place? What does it mean to have "open space" in school or classroom?

17. Samaya (Parent and the Teacher)

What is the "barrier" between parents and teachers in schools? What would happen if it went away?

18. Navajo School (How Miracles Happen)

Is it the job of the school to pass along local and ethnic culture? What is the role of the school in the community?

19. Still We Wander

Have we accidentally re-engineered our classroom methodologies to exclude students who don't learn like the teachers we hire? As we narrow the role and definition of classroom teacher, what kinds of learning and knowing are we losing?

20. Pete Seeger: A Real Teacher

Is there such a thing as authentic teaching or authentic learning? How far can the teacher go to move instruction toward authentic accomplishments for students?

21. The Wounded Ones (A Winter Night With No Lights)

Working with teens, how do we treat the dark ones? To what extent do conformity and "standard" expectations force our students to lose their way?

22. Zenbells (The Art of Paying Attention)
Is "Alright, quiet down over there," achieving what we want—and what presumptions does this command reveal in educators? Are educators and parents using much of what we know about consciousness and concentration? What is more essential to great teaching: providing great information or creating a great environment for learning?

23. The Gaokao Cowboy
How can we make every class like a lab where genuine discovery is possible? Is our role as teachers and parents to help kids fit in or stand out? And should America be more like China?

24. Too Nice a Day to Stay Inside
What could be the best roles and purposes for free time in the classroom and the school day? What if we could restore play as a fundamental way of learning in the classroom?

25. Tree Stumps
What new kinds of classroom organizations might we try? Would teaching in natural spaces result in a different kind of human development? What can we do with these possibilities?

26. What Do We Care About?
Is there a difference between Eastern and Western purposes for schooling? As the east and the west emulate each other, what is lost?

28. Boulder
If people are essentially self-interested, can they have a global perspective? Is the teacher's job more essentially to talk or to listen?

27. Han (Happiness as a Measurable Educational Outcome)
What if we assigned, benchmarked, taught, and measured student happiness in school: Graded it, paid teachers for it, and ranked school systems by it?

29. Education in the Real World
What presumptions about "normal" schools are holding us back?

30. What the Revolution Looks Like
When was the last time you had a great conversation with a teen? To what extent do teachers risk their jobs to do this? Would you risk a job as a teacher in pursuit of great conversations?

31. Find Your People
What are we doing to give our students a sense of real belongingness in the classroom and around the campuses of America? Is the teacher's fundamental allegiance to the school system . . . or to their students?

32. The Manhasset Indians (Lacrosse and the Real History of Comprehensive Schools in America)
Does bussing work? 25 million American students now go on 10 billion, socially questionable school bus trips per year. What could we get back if we had local community schools again? What are the unintended impacts of school consolidation?

33. Bigness (We've Got to Fight, Boys)
To what extent do we all presume the stature of "bigness" in America?

34. The Black Horse of Tahiti
Are the measurable goals in student achievement more valuable than the immeasurable ones? To what extent do we expect teachers to pass along our culture?

35. Indians of Six Nations
Are basic survival skills and living off the land worth teaching about? Who will teach them?

36. The Moon in a Jar
What unconscious beliefs from our own early lives now guide the behaviors, emotions, and thoughts we have as educators? How can we be better listeners?

37. A Refugee
What keeps us in this work?

Sugata Mitra joins an "evolving fishbowl" at the annual International Democratic Education Conference, 2013.

Acknowledgements

Thank you to the many characters in this book who allowed me to engage with them openly, often across huge cultural gulfs; some of you will see your names in these pages and others may recognize yourselves or aspects of yourselves through pseudonyms. Thanks to Joe Brooks of Community Works Journal, Melissa Greenwood of SmartBriefs in Education, Michael Brosnan and Ari Pinkus of Independent Schools magazine, Jerry Mintz of Alternative Educators Resource Organization (AERO), whose publications covered many of these ideas in their developing stages. With appreciation for Welsh author Jay Griffiths and American organizational theorist and author Meg Wheatley who's ideas keep transforming my own—and thanks, Meg, for passing along some of the transformational poems found in these pages. Thanks to Lori Gertz (and Freakin' Genius Marketing) and to Kenneth Kales (and Kales Publishing) for deep editing of the collection as a whole, the fine-tuning, and the sage advice you each gave. Thanks to Alicia Tembi of the Small Schools Coalition, for supporting and advancing our understanding of small schools and their extraordinary value. Credit goes to student Skyler Pia for the "khaki" quote in the story "Boulder." Thanks to Doug Katz for your ever-wise consultations. And thanks to Johnny King for photo editing. Many thanks to Bill Harman for your wisdom and for sharing your worldwide network of friends, some of whom appear herein. Thank-you to loyal reader/critics Sally Grauer, Audrey Grauer, Susan Nestor, Christina Burress, Kevin Wirick and many others. And special thanks to Isaac Graves who worked tirelessly to get this edited, designed, and published.